USA or Bust ©™

I was interviewed twice by KGO News Radio in San Francisco. They gave me great coverage before and during my trip. Thank you. Also thanks goes out to the Santa Cruz Sentinel and the Press Banner for their newspaper coverage, and to Abigail for her editorial and proofreading skills. Most of all, I want to thank my family and friends for giving me encouragement and couches to sleep on. I apologize to those I interviewed and photographed but did not include in this book. The reasons range from space constraints to redundancy issues. And finally, I want to thank everyone who participated for their patience and input. This book would not exist without them.

Atomic Drop Press First Edition Book ■ 2014 © J.W. Zook

Based on the original limited edition hardcover *USA or Bust* © 2009

ISBN 978-0-9827669-7-2

Atomic Drop Press

USA or Bust

America at the Crossroads

J.W. Zook

The 5th Anniversary Edition

I combed through the original book and made a few minor edits, as well as, reprocessing the photographs and repositioning a few of them to fit the newer format. With these minor exceptions this is a faithful reproduction of the original 2009 publication.

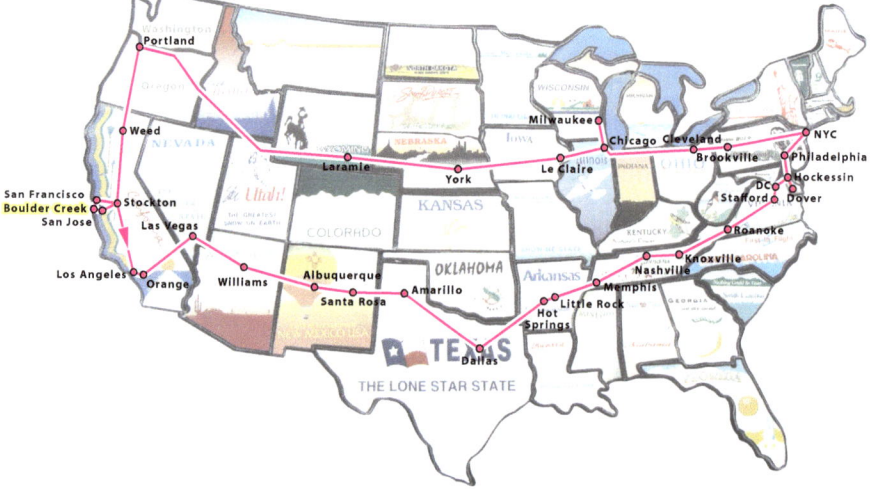

For Julia

Contents

Fifth Anniversary **Foreword**

In 2009 I drove around the United States in my search for America. The journey occurred with a new President in office, the country teetering on the brink of economic collapse, bogged down in two dubious wars, and growing political adversity. I decided to revisit that journey by republishing *USA or Bust* with Atomic Drop Press. The more things change, the more they stay the same. But they do change.

Some of those changes are of a more personal nature: my daughter, Julia, is long out of high school and finishing up college, my neighbors, Geoff and Laura, have since moved to lovely digs in Oregon, Amanda and Kevin are now married and raising their daughter in their new home, Heather and J. Paul, too, are now married, Don is no longer the lone population of Buford, Wyoming, and three dear people (one I knew my whole life, one I knew briefly, and one was a close friend of a close friend) have died. There have been other weddings, other births, and other deaths. Life's dance continues and everybody has a story. Some are still unfolding, some have reached their final chapter.

The arch bridge near the Hoover Dam has been completed. It was in the midst of construction when I drove over the dam on my way eastward. 1 World Trade Center is now a shining jewel in New York City's crown. Only the foundation existed when I last visited. Coming back west I drove over the San Francisco-Oakland Bay Bridge—a drive I used to make on a daily basis years earlier—it too has changed with a new, more earthquake-proof eastern span.

The economy still rests on a shaky footing and the political climate is as combative as ever. Our nation, and the world, remains locked in socioeconomic doldrums even as events appear poised for strife. History has eras of dark and light. And only history can hold our time and people in full judgment.

Reading through my thoughts from a half-decade earlier, I find most of them still timely and valid. But as things change, so do minds and social climates. Like all things, the United States is in constant flux, searching for a sense of stability without standing still. We are a nation that believes we were born in perfection looking for improvement. And there are many miles to go.

Have we been here before? Certainly. A cursory understanding of U.S. history tells us that there have been several contentious and challenging periods. As of late, there's a small mean-spirited element within our borders that feels absolutely entitled to crush the hearts, minds, and spirits of the vast majority. And that majority, at times, seems to be working against its own self-interest. Some seem to be impervious to the common good and well-considered reason. Whatever happened to: United we stand, divided we fall? And: He ain't heavy, he's my brother? Helping others help themselves is not a crime. It is a blessing. When did compromise become an invective? A loud minority see life as their way or the highway. And it was to this highway that I took to compile this book. I hoped for the best, while planning for the worst, and I was often surprised. I had nothing but rewarding, engaging experiences with the people I met along the way.

Something that clearly *was* changing, even when I first attempted to publicize the book five years ago, was the erosion and downsizing of print media—and this was before the existence of the iPad. The speed of technology's pace is the one great exception to things not changing. A book today demands that it be digital as well as print. The avenues of publicity have changed, too. The local station that gave me some fine publicity during my original drive has changed hands and I doubt that the present version of this San Francisco institution would have paid me any notice.

Coordinating time and money is always one of life's great balancing acts. When you're busy making money, there's usually no time to travel. And when you have the time, the money's not there. I had two months where I was blessed with both money and time. In re-reading the book, I still stand by my impressions of the people and places I had the great fortune to meet and visit.

J.W. Zook
July 4, 2014

Original **Introduction**

For several years I've been pestering my family and friends with two questions: "Do you think there could be another Great Depression?" And, "Isn't it time for a new Works Progress Administration?"

The first question was usually met with a resounding, "No." There were too many checks and balances. Times had changed; we were beyond that. Besides, what could go wrong? The second was answered by an unenthusiastic, "Yes." Our nation's roads, bridges, and dams all need work. Everyone agreed. Something had to be done. But what could we do? My family and friends were very tolerant of my apparent obsession with dire concerns for the near future. And the thing is, I consider myself a positive guy. So where was my sense of alarm coming from?

When events seemed to have caught up with my obsession, I decided I could not wait for a resurgence of the WPA or a related program, the FSA (Farm Security Administration), whose mission then was, in part, to document the plight of the 1930s through photography and writing. I knew that I had to go out on my own. The idea of driving around our country and interviewing, photographing, and writing about America and Americans during our current crisis just seemed right. A road trip was in order.

The whole plan gelled in mid-February, 2009. A new President was in office and hope was on the uptick, even if the economy wasn't. The United States was fighting two wars abroad, and along with the collapse of the housing market and its cascading effect on business and finance, things were taking their toll.

Beginning on September 11, 2001 this country changed. The wounds of that terrible day have yet to heal. They may never fully heal. We seem to be floundering. What unites us as a nation? What are our hopes, struggles, and dreams? With the statistics of the 2010 census due about the time of this book's publication, I can only hope that these photos and interviews add flesh and form to dry facts and figures. Behind every number stands a very real person.

Many days started with a long drive. I would stop when I came to a city or town that appeared to be a target-rich environment. Diners, bars, shopping malls—all were great places for people to speak their minds. And they did. After all, this is America. Everyone has an opinion. Everybody has a story. And if one picture is worth a thousand words and one word is also worth a thousand pictures, then the marriage of pictures and words tells the story best.

Besides the portraits and interviews, I've included ancillary images and support material. No topic was off limits. I did my best to make people feel relaxed, so they would open up about the circumstances of their lives and the times they live in.

As of this writing the news is beginning to fill with reports of an economic rebound. Has the whole mess really played out?

We'll see.

No matter, the photographs and interviews stand on their own as a testament to our daily lives.

E pluribus unum—Out of many one. Individual voices blended together creating a singular, rich chorus. United we stand, of thee I sing...

J.W. Zook
September 2009

All interviews and photo sessions took place between the months of March and July and are displayed in this book roughly in the order in which they occurred. My actual road trip began on April 29th (President Obama's 100th day in office) and ended on June 26—fifty-nine days and twenty-three states later. I used only first names for privacy reasons.

Santa Cruz, California

James

I've known James for over thirty years. I first met him when he was coming off a stint as a cowboy on his family's ranch. He is a vexillologist (flag expert), historian, raconteur, and Boy Scout leader. His home is in Reno, Nevada with his wife and son. I interviewed him in his office in Santa Cruz, California, where he is Chief Curator for the Zaricor Flag Collection.

I worked for many years at The Flag Store in San Francisco until 1989. That year I returned to Nevada and went back to graduate school pursuing a teaching credential. Then I interrupted grad school to come back to the flag industry. I stayed from 1992 to 1996 when that flag store was sold, then I returned to Nevada in 1997 and finished my credential. I taught for a year, high school. I was also a substitute teacher, I did middle school and high school. In 2003 I took some Cub Scouts to see a museum exhibit at the Presidio in San Francisco. I was correcting some of the gallery copy in the exhibition. And that led me to Mr. Zaricor and his collection of these flags. I've been curating his collection since then.

I'm essentially a consultant, so the economy really hasn't affected me. Technically, if the Feds wanted to count me, I'd be unemployed—or self-employed. I'm not actually seeking an outside job, so I'm not in the ranks of the unemployed, but I'm not really employed in the traditional sense. My time is my own. I come down here (Santa Cruz) as needed. I still live in Reno, but I come down here generally ten days to two weeks at a whack. I help with whatever it is we are working on with the collection.

So the economy has been neither good nor bad to me, but the economy has affected the flag market. I'm not involved in sales in a retail environment, but we monitor all the flags that are sold at auction in the United States. For example, I was doing research this morning and discovered that a Union Jack sold in the United Kingdom for 40,000 Pounds in November of 2007. That's a flag I want to track. Flags from that era, the 18th century, are quite rare, so now we have a marker to use to value the collection.

Most flags are sold at auction and that's a collectors' market, rather than a commodities market. The rule of supply and demand doesn't apply, because the supply of antique flags is quite finite. So, the more you buy the more that pool is diminished. It has the effect of driving the prices up. There is a collectors' market, people that acquire old flags, then sell them for personal reasons, never to be displayed. Mr. Zaricor's collection is a little different; he uses his collection as a working collection. It's available for research and exhibition.

My wife works for a company that does payroll. She deals with state governments a lot in the payment and collection on the tax side. Her situation hasn't really been affected yet, however, as the layoffs continue in large industries, there may be less need for payroll services. Some companies may streamline, so there's a potential.

And my teen son, he's aware of the fact that there's an economic downturn, but he's in school and still really dependent upon us for his support. He turns sixteen shortly. Let me give you an idea of how much this *hasn't* affected him. He's been looking through fliers for Ferraris, not wanting to drive my old van—which he wouldn't be seen dead in.

The economy has affected some people I know, who have been laid off. In Nevada, except for people in the housing industry, no one's been hit very hard. The people in mining, especially gold mining, are enjoying a boom, because gold prices have been up, so parts of the state have relatively low unemployment.

Nevada was one of the fastest-growing states for housing, so now foreclosures are very high, especially in Clark County, which is southern Nevada, but also in the Reno area. They suffered from the housing bubble, but that was across the country, and was not necessarily confined to there. Reno and Las Vegas were enjoying an unprecedented growth period, so the housing industry was booming. There was a lot of overbuilding, so those industries are suffering in the general economic downturn.

The prices of houses were very reasonable, that's why Nevada was very attractive to Californians. California's confiscatory tax structure has driven a lot of wealth out of California. Nevada has a much less stringent tax structure and has no state income tax. It's a destination state for some, as long as there's employment. It's a double-edged sword.

Two things that helped cause the downturn were there was an oversupply of houses and there was easy credit for people that probably weren't qualified. There was no oversight and there was a political will to put unqualified people into houses. With the combination of bad mortgages and overbuilding, the bubble burst. Not everybody should own a house.

This is an aberration, and the market will recover. The question people are asking is, "Will we suffer through a depression as severe as the one in the 1930s?" The answer is that I don't know. My gut feeling is no, but I don't know. Economists don't know what triggered the other one. Generally, we accept that the stock market triggered it. No one's really identified whether it was monetary policies, whether it was Keynesian, or was capital in the wrong places. Economist and scholars are still debating it. We were a more agrarian economy and people took it in stride. The question is, if we did have a situation like that would we survive today? Again the answer is, I don't know.

I see a lot of signs of an entitlement mentality, rather than a can-do mentality—not only in my acquaintances, but also in my son's peers. Everybody wants a position, no one wants a job anymore. I know when I was in graduate school, finding a job working in a prep kitchen or finding a job working for a construction company packing two-by-fours was easy to do. It was a one-phone call problem, but I see people unwilling to do that. Now that may change if the downturn lengthens. Is all the government action going to mitigate it? Probably in the short term, but this can't be sustained, because I don't think you can spend your way out of the problem. You can't extract wealth from the productive part of your economy and give it to the nonproductive part by make-work jobs. Sooner or later you run out of other people's money to spend. As Milton Freedman said, "The printing press is so much easier to extort than the people."

There's a fear of using the word "Depression." Rather than avoiding that D-word, we can just call it another D-word "Downturn," but there have been other periods. The so-called Great Depression really lasted from October of 1929—the trigger was the stock market collapse—until it bottomed out in 1933, then there was a recovery to the 1929 prices, but there wasn't a return of consumer confidence. There was a downturn in 1937 and probably it was the government spending contingent with World War II that brought about a recovery for the whole world. In fact, it's funny, people compare the industrialized West with Russia during the Great Depression, and point out that Russia didn't suffer from the Great Depression, but while that's true, I don't think it was because of anything inherently superior in the Marxist system, but rather the fact that they were recovering from a bloody and protracted civil war, and pretty much had removed themselves from the world economy. By ideology and isolation, the West had helped complement that philosophy, so though they were essentially self-contained, they were all primarily in an agrarian economy. Stalin was able to use that lull to make the Five-Year Plans work. He took the second-most backward nation and turned it into one of the most powerful in a short time, but I don't know that that's the model we want to emulate to recover from this downturn.

Are we probably going to have to make some changes? I absolutely think so. I don't know that we can continue to consume at the present rate. It's a question of want versus need. Do we really need all this stuff? And the answer is probably not. Do we want it? Of course we're going to continue to want it as long as it's marketed to us. It's the age-old thing. It's like the difference between a rainforest and a jungle. The answer is marketing. Does everybody really *need* a fifty-two-inch flat-screen TV? No. That's the whole bread-and-circus thing. Can we bring enough grain back from Egypt to feed the people of Rome? Well, no. Then we should bring back the sand for the chariot track, because we can entertain the people with games, so we can make them forget about the fact that they have no bread. You can draw parallels with America's fascination with sports and ancient Rome's. Gibbon in his landmark *Decline and Fall of the Roman Empire,* gives the three reasons for Rome's collapse as defense spending—the cost of keeping all those legions in the field—welfare, and a preoccupation with sports. Thank God we have none of that.

There's also the cyclical nature of history—the theory that the dreams of a revolution only last eight generations. The generation that spawned the revolution is imbued with the revolutionary principles, and they can pass that on to their children and grandchildren, and that takes care of the first three generations. So, the grandchildren are the last contact with the first generation, so in theory there's a connection from the third generation to the fourth and fifth and sixth generations, so by the seventh generation there's no direct contact with the founders, and by the eighth generation you have collapse. That generally happens at about two hundred to two hundred and fifty years.

We're the Saudi Arabia of coal, but we don't want to burn coal because, oh my God, there's pollution. It's a trade-off. I keep wondering, what exactly is a *green* job? You hear that we're going to save three million green jobs. I'd just like to know what that is. The new Chief of Staff for the President said, "I never want to see a crisis go to waste." There is an ideology behind all of this. I think there's a radical departure from what the role of government has traditionally been in the United States. I think Obama has socially active ideas on the European model, but he's not a socialist in the pure Marxist sense. Finland is a socialist country. Sweden is a socialist country. The problem is that we could do that, but we have to do it through the ballot box—not through fiat; not through executive order. So, if that's the path we want to take, then that's what I think we should do. For example, all this nonsense about health care spending. Well, if that's what we wanted—if we want the government to provide health care, then we should put it in the Constitution, but right now the government is not charged with that. They're to provide the common defense and promote the general welfare—not provide it. The Constitution's a living, working document, because they left us the mechanism to change it. The answer is that we have a chance to have a revolution in this country every four years. And, if you think of some elections, this past one people are pointing to as a radical change in administrations, but I would submit that the 1860 election was even more radical—where we had an absolute and complete change of philosophy to the point of force of arms in the form of a civil war. So, we can have dramatic and sweeping change in the United States through the ballot box. The thing about the recent Obama administration is that the world stands in awe of us for having the ability for a peaceful change of power with two gentlemen who do not see eye-to-eye. We saw it before—Carter to Reagan, Clinton to Bush, and now we've seen it in

Bush to Obama. Very few countries can make the same claim. You look at the European democracies—the government of France fell because of a taxi strike. I really do think that our government is strong enough to survive this downturn—and the current administration. If the stimulus package doesn't work, he will be a one-term President.

We always want to level the playing field, but there's nothing in the Constitution about fairness. Equity before the law, yes, but fairness, no. It's true that we're all created equal, but the sad reality is that we don't stay that way. Some of us are just better at things than others. What I bristle at is, I really don't think that spreading the misery around is what the founders had in mind. What I think is that through your own efforts, intellect, and hard work you can rise to your own greatest level. That's what the American Dream is. The goal should be to get government out of your way.

[About the war in Iraq.] There was never a good war or a bad peace. Wether the army should be used for social programs is a separate issue. I personally think it should not. The purpose of an army is to get people to break things. The Center for Strategic Studies says the United States can fight one and a half wars. China could fight three wars. Russia two and a half. That's where we make up for it with technology. The question is, can we sustain it? I think the Falklands War proved that technology may not be the answer, when a hundred-thousand-dollar missile can sink a billion-dollar ship.

It's important to remember that in the Great Seal of the United States the eagle holds two things: in one talon he holds a bundle of arrows, symbolic of defense, and in the other he holds an olive branch, which is what everybody misunderstands. If you read the text accompanying the Great Seal, the olive branch stands for the power of peace. That's why the eagle looks to the olive branch. That's the direction it prefers. So maybe we should give the power of peace a try, but we should not let go of the arrows.

The Christian right in this country is, in my opinion, misinterpreting their holy book, because Jesus said, "There are only two commandments: Have no other gods before me and love your neighbor as you would love yourself." Those are the two greatest commandments. The others are handy, but they're in the Old Testament. So, if you're a Christian you subscribe to the principles of Christ—you walk around in the club that bears his name, so maybe they ought to look at his commandments. Remember, we're a secular nation. We're a deist nation. It says in the Declaration of Independence, "Endowed by our creator with certain inalienable rights." And in the Constitution it says, "Done this day, the year of our Lord." So our two founding documents founded us as a deist nation. We're not a Christian nation. Religion, as we know it, was organized by man. It is a kind of a club. As the great theologian, Kirby J. Hensley once said, the problem with religions is that they believe they're the only door to salvation, yet in reality, probably all of them are. And they all have the Golden Rule. Well, I'm not sure about atheists. We were created as a deist nation—that was the intent of the founding fathers. There's nothing in the Constitution about being offended. We've become such a nation of whiners. ■

San Jose, California

Tiyasha

Tiyasha's a Youth Intervention Worker with the Restorative Justice Program in San Jose, California. She works hard to keep youthful offenders from sinking further into the criminal justice system.

For people like us, the recovery is not happening fast enough. People are getting further and further down, and it's hard to climb back up. People used to live at a certain level of luxuries—it's not even luxuries any more, it's necessities. That's what's missing. Programs are getting cut, food banks are going dry. Where are they supposed to get their money from?

[About a food program and kitchen at a local church.] There're less people at the beginning of the month, but the last week of the month people come more and more. And we don't actually work there anymore. No. Because the kids needed to have a TB [tuberculosis] clearance—something really hard for most of the kids to have access to. The TB was at their own cost. The kitchen always tells us to come back. We had a good experience there. I miss that place.

My hours are so varied right now. I sometimes just go home and go to sleep. I barely have time to unwind or anything.

In the last few years, we've actually seen an increase in property offenses in our youth. From last year, November, these citations happened about five, six months prior to them coming to our program. We've been having an influx of property crimes, from shoplifting to stealing things, more often than other crimes that we usually have. It indicates that the parents aren't able to provide for their kids the things that they want. Usually it's clothes, jewelry…things that they used to get pocket money for. They're teenagers; they're spoiled. They want their iPhones, iPod, the latest fashions. You can't be left behind. If everyone is having it, you have to have it.

I teach a drug and alcohol class. We've seen a decrease in kids getting referred to us. My class used to be more alcohol and weed—now it's more weed. So, I don't know if these trends mean anything. These are just things that I've noticed. Weed's easier to get. There's been a crackdown on alcohol. Just legalizing weed will make it not as amazing as it is. Right now it's forbidden fruit. I just hope that some of the kids going through my program somehow make it into future legislation and change that. They can see firsthand how ridiculous it is.

We did a fund-raiser at the beginning of April and the problem was that the adults attending the event were saying the same thing: They don't have any money to give. Even though it's a great cause. We had a fashion show and auction. Everyone had a great time, but when we went back and asked for funds, it just didn't happen. We were thinking of hitting up all the high-tech companies, but it was one thing after another. These people are getting laid off and this company's laying people off. I don't think I can ask these people for money.

The economy is definitely a confidence-related thing. At the same time, there's only so much that Obama can say. He's just one guy. It's hard to do that leap of faith when everyone around you is getting laid off. I feel at this point I might get laid off soon. I'm starting to hold onto my money. I can feel it. We're going to have a sixty-four percent cut in our budget and I don't know how we're going to survive that. State funding was cut only five percent, which isn't too bad. Locally, San Jose is doing the sixty-four percent cut to our budget and reassigning it to juvenile hall. We were trying for our events to get sponsored, but there's a lot of competition out there. Now organizations are being very specific about what you can use the money for.

It's been going this way for a while. I remember my dad saying it can't keep going up—like the housing market. It had to come down. They were ridiculous amounts. Everyone is hoping for the best, but at the rate it's going right now, there's not much hope. Thankfully, I'm still living with my parents. I'm thinking about my car payment and health insurance. And those are the kind of things you need in a society like this. Once you start losing those, where do you go from there? That's when you turn to violence. It starts going the wrong way.

We don't get really high-crime kids. We realize there's more gang activity as of late. We've actually had to kick some kids out of our program because it got so bad that they fought in front of us. I've never seen that. I've never seen the Norteños versus Sureños. Kids are just wearing more colors and being more obvious about it and not really caring. I don't know if it's lack of parenting or…I don't know what it is, because definitely since January we've seen a spike in it. They're so involved in instilling that respect—but what about respect for life. But they don't have jobs and they have nothing to do. They get very influenced. I've had a lot kids saying they needed to get a job. It's not looking good.

Our grant writers are trying, but it looks like our program will change. They're thinking that we have to expand to house more post-juvenile-hall kids, so after they finish their contract at the hall they can do some sort of service with us. But then, you start mixing in first-time offenders with juvy kids and it's not the best environment. Then they get friendly and then they think that, oh, that person survived juvy, I can do it. I can do some hard crimes and get out. They need to be separated. People behind desks don't get that. They're not out there in front with community service, seeing how kids are influenced. ■

San Jose, California

Julia

For a teenage perspective on the economy, I interviewed my favorite daughter, Julia. She was weeks away from graduating high school and desperately looking for a summer job.

This one job told me to call their hotline. The couple of times I've called, it's always full. Technically, I'm hired, and their first show is in a week and a half. I'll be an usher. I show them to their seats. I'm looking forward to Blazed and Confused—that's Snoop Dogg and Slightly Stoopid—and the Warp Tour.

I've been looking for work for five months. It's not going too well. I passed out fifty resumes and the only thing I can get are part-time summer jobs. I tried downtown and some of the big businesses, but also little mom and pop places. Nobody's really hiring.

Julia did finally accept some part-time work for a national clothing chain. She's also been able to usher at a few concerts at a well-known outdoor venue.

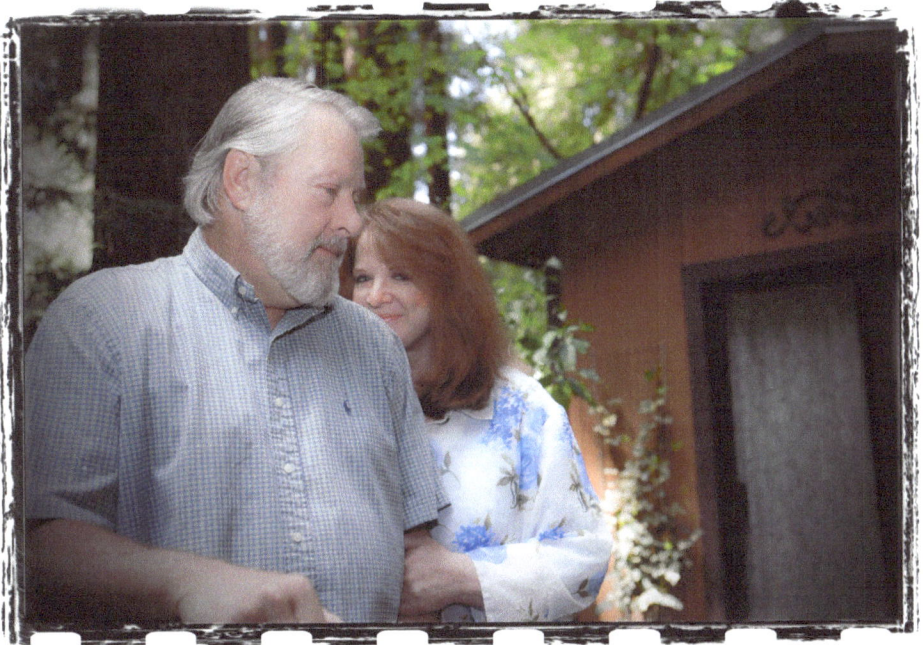

Boulder Creek, California

Geoff and Laura

Geoff and Laura live next door to me. They've been good neighbors and friends. Geoff has worked largely as a construction foreman. He is a Vietnam vet. Laura is a freelance graphic designer and works from home. They've been sweethearts since high school and married forever.

Geoff: Being a construction superintendent, and having been employed for over thirty years straight, it came as a surprise that my contractor didn't want to carry me on to another job. But he didn't have another estate job to put me on and I'd already told him that I was thinking about retirement. And being almost sixty years of age turned out to be a detriment, because he had other younger men to fill in on that, so I was laid off. There wasn't too much hope of me coming back, so I looked around for other work, but construction, with the economy taking a real downturn, was one of the first things to really get hit. People stopped doing projects and they weren't doing the type of projects I had been working on which were these estate projects. This was early 2007. March was when I was let off. Even the other contractors were looking for younger men to fill the positions, so age started working against me.

But that was okay. I was thinking that I would be able to start retiring on my IRA money, so I took a chance on that, but I used up some of it. And that was when the economy started really turning down and the market started really going, then all of a sudden my IRA money became half of what it was.

I'm only sitting okay because of a twist of fate. I had my mother passing on, otherwise I would be in very bad shape—being unemployed without too much hope of being employed in the same field at the same rate that I was at. Using my IRA money, but knowing that my mother, who was aging, at ninety years of age, at some point would pass away, and that she and my father had saved money, because they were Depression-Era babies and saved everything, so that there was good money that my brother and I were able to split, which now makes it financially easier for me to think of the future.

Laura: Or I'd have to go back to work.

Geoff: I think a lot of Baby Boomers are going to be in the same boat, in the sense that if their parents haven't passed away, that they're going to be passing away soon, and that there will be a whole lot more people that will inherit, which will provide at least a security for retirement of sorts.

There's a lot of people in the market. There's a lot of unemployment. There's a whole lot more young people out there; not only that, they're more willing to work…

Laura: For ten dollars an hour. Graphic artists, web designers…

Geoff: It's a generational thing. Even we complained about our parents. We were all for cultural change and now our children and the next generation is all changed again, but they're all tech savvy compared to what were are. We're all back at the typewriter stage. In my case, photographic stage with film. The world's gotten much smaller because of communication, because of the Internet. Everybody's next door now.

The mode of travel before in our parents' generation—most of the people never went thirty miles from the home where they were born. During the Depression they didn't even have cars. My grandfather, who was a doctor, he was accepting trade, such as chickens and bags of potatoes.

Laura: I've gotten less work in the last couple of years. For fun I do the eBay thing.

Geoff: It's not that people buying less on eBay, it's just that there's more hard bargaining. It doesn't even make it profitable to try and sell anything. There's too much time and effort to package up anything and sell it. People want to pay pennies for anything now. Before, it was a fad for collectors to try and find items, but that's all gone now. The easy money's all gone now.

Everybody's just going to have to learn to cut back. I think we're lucky in the sense that I learned from my father to be a saver at least. At my company, the opportunity arose to get 401Ks, and Laura had already had the opportunity at Apple, and we had taken advantage of it when she was young. That savings is now making it possible. And it never seemed to matter that much in my paycheck. When it was being saved, it was either give it to the government or give it to myself, so that was an easy solution. It was painless savings that now has paid off. Saving is simple and at the time it was a bull market, so the money I saved doubled. It went down when the market went down, but I was ahead of the game and was able to pull some out at the time and reinvest in other things, so that wasn't as painful.

Laura: We've turned into thrift store junkies. I've picked up some hundred-dollar shirts for Geoff for eight or nine dollars.

Geoff: We were trying to live within our means when were getting our first house. We could have bought more house, but it would have put us in a range where it would have made payments a whole lot harder.

Laura: Both of us would have had to work for thirty years.

Geoff: By living below our means a little bit, I was able to save. And in saving it's paid off. We consumed, but we weren't heavy consumers that had to have every new gadget.

Laura: Yeah, we cut back on our desires.

Geoff: We didn't have every toy that came out.

Laura: And we didn't travel for years.

Geoff: Now we have the time. We've saved up some money. Now we can hopefully enjoy it at an age when we're not too old to enjoy it.

Laura: But we're cutting it kind of close.

Geoff: [Laughs.] And we don't have any children, so we don't have anybody to leave it to other than brothers, nieces, and nephews. We don't have to worry about saving money for our heirs.

Laura: We're trying to time it just right. ■

University of the Pacific — Stockton, California

Along Interstate 5, California

Stockton, California

Will

Will came to the United States from Argentina with his parents when he was four-years old. He is a published author and lover of books. He runs his own bookstore out of his home, thanks to the Internet. His wife, Agnes, is a real estate appraiser. She is currently back in school working on a degree in psychology. I've known both of them for a very long time. Lively debates always ensue when we visit one another. Neither one wanted to commit to being photographed. Agnes did not want to be interviewed.

You look at all art, everything: our music, our books, our movies, everything is so fucking dull.

The sixties didn't seem to have a literary component like the fifties did.

No. By that time the interest in a literary scene had died in America. The sixties was about the music.

How's the bookstore doing?

Pretty slow. Pretty slow. I'm still getting a fairly normal amount of orders, but cheaper books. I'm not selling too much high-end stuff. Sometimes I'm astounded. I don't have that many cheap books in the store, but some days that's all I'll sell. It's all through other vendors on the Internet.

[Later.] You take everybody you and I know, we all grew up in modest-sized homes. Almost everyone I know grew up in a house that was anywhere between a thousand and fifteen hundred square feet max. And that would have been a big home back then. The most significant thing I find when I go into older houses is the size of the closet. Closets used to be very, very small—tiny little things. Garages, for the most part, were one-car garages. And if you had a two-car garage, two cars barely fit. Now today, we used to go to open houses a lot and see model homes, closets are bigger than the old bedrooms. People have these enormous closets. They have, of course, the walk-in closets in the master bedroom. There're lots of closets all over the house. The garages are immense, and yet there's a storage facility on every street corner in modern America. People somehow need an additional thousand square feet just to store their stuff. That's the amazing thing to me; we always seem to need new stuff. And another thing about when we grew up is that with most of our parents only our dads worked. And if mothers did work, it was a part-time job they'd take temporarily because they wanted to buy a color TV, a car, or something…and yet most of our parents…most were union workers. I remember my dad, he got his vacation, medical, retirement, and we weren't poor. That's the amazing thing, to think that one income could have done that. Today, most people with both parents working full-time are still having a hard time making ends meet.

From my perspective, the sort of person I am, I don't want to extend all my energy towards just making money. And again, during those good times we were fortunate enough to grow up in, it was just a forty-hour-a-week job. You just didn't sweat it.

[About Stockton being the foreclosure capital of the nation.] The other day Ag [Agnes] appraised a little house—about nine-hundred square feet—here in Stockton for $45,000. I think Stockton is like third, Detroit passed it, and I think Las Vegas. Phoenix may have passed it, too.

When Ag and I took our trip about four years ago, Phoenix was just endless. It was an infinite-sized city. Vegas was the same way. We went to Vegas the first year we were together and then sixteen years later we went back—it was unrecognizable. It had swelled.

You know how there is a group of people that believe that peak oil is upon us. And their nightmare scenario is that our cities will be like Phoenix and Las Vegas, because no one will be able to live there anymore. We won't be able to have the power… But it's amazing, there's one up here near Sacramento called Elk Grove that went from nothing to a city about the size of Stockton in a few years and it's massive. [In just nine years the population has gone from 59,984 to an estimated 136,000.]

It used to be that in California everything was more expensive, but now the infection has spread throughout the whole country. I remember that for years when I would talk to Edgeman [a mutual friend who lives in Texas], we were paying fifty cents more for gasoline than he was. Our PG&E was double his. It was ridiculous. Just because of the geography we're paying an insane amount of extra money.

There's a book called *Valley of the Moon,* by Jack London. It's not a great book, but every Californian needs to read it. The first couple of hundred pages are about a couple struggling in the unions…but the last couple of hundred pages of it, they get fed up and they decide to take a walking tour of California to find the ideal place to live. And it is stunning. It was written back in 1908, 1911, somewhere in the first twenty years of that century, before World War I [it was published in 1913] and it's just fabulous. You recognize everywhere they go, but it's a totally different world.

I don't know if we are going to recover from this in our lifetime. What they're doing, Geithner and Sumner and those boys, at best they're putting a Band-Aid on the problem. They might right it for a brief spell, but they're just setting up for a bigger fall. But, I don't know, Obama… the thing about Obama is that he's obviously very intelligent, and he's obviously not like George Bush, who hides from the world. All his aides were instructed not to tell him stuff. I get the feeling that Obama keeps his eyes peeled. He reads. And why did he ignore all the intelligentsia in America who were all warning him specifically about hiring Sumner. The other people they cautioned against Geithner. What made him do this? What exactly was the thought process? Why does he continue to stick with them as they clearly continue to drive our economy deeper in the toilet? It's very puzzling.

In the 1930s they put in all these safeguards. But they've been stripped away. What kind of nut or self-delusional idiot could buy into the notion that big business and the market will regulate itself? It's like swimming up to a shark and petting it, thinking the shark isn't going to hurt me. It's the nature of business to always make more money. If you don't put the brakes on—just let them go their own way—there isn't this happy medium where competition keeps everybody on an even keel. It's dog-eat-dog. The big eat the small. As there're more and more big companies and less and less small ones, there's less options.

There was that thing where it was crucial to bail out the banks. The argument they used was that we need the banks to loan you money. But it's utterly irrelevant whether they're loaning out money, because nobody wants to borrow any at this point. People are up to their necks in debt. They're losing their houses; they're losing their jobs. Nobody's willing to take out a loan.

They have figured it out. They take it from wherever they can. And the thing is, if you only have to pay the Fed a quarter percent for this money you're still going to take it out on your credit card holders. That's just the way business operates. You heard that expression: How can you privatize profit and socialize loss? They've figured it out that they're being allowed to do that. It's never going to cross their minds not to.

I love the fact that we're always reminded that we're a country of great entrepreneurs. That's the American spirit. So why do we always shortchange that at a time like this? If Ford, GM, and Chrysler went out of business, there'd be three new upstarts hiring those people back. There's the Smart Car that Ford is building—that little tiny thing, and it starts at $16,000. Why? You can buy a *real* car that gives you just as good mileage and they sell for less. It'd be nice to buy American and help our fellow citizens. We never set out to buy Hyundai or Honda. We compared value. But a comparable American car a) costs much more, and b) they were rated far lower. ■

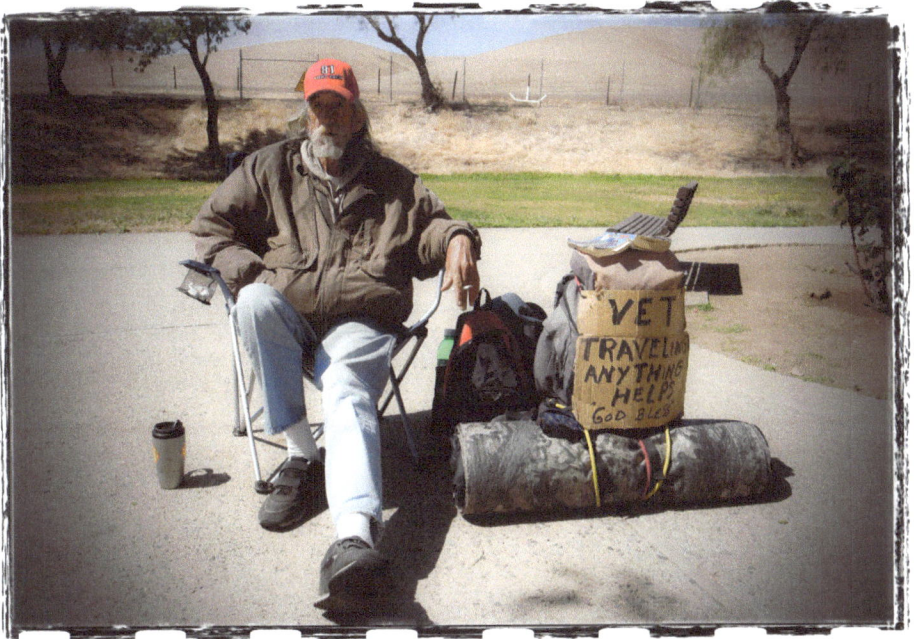

Interstate 5, California

Mike

I met "Miner" Mike (cover photo) traveling south on Interstate 5 in California. With a cozy set-up—chair, book, coffee, and backpack—he was a man in no hurry. He had a sign reading: "Vet. Traveling. Anything helps. God bless." He gets by on his VA benefits, gold panning, and the kindness of strangers.

My friends all call me "Miner" 'cause I gold mine and teach gold mining in Northern California, Oregon, Idaho, and around the country. There's more gold out there than people have a clue. Most people don't know much about it. There are fifty states in the United States, and of that fifty states, what people don't understand is that thirty-nine of them are gold-bearing states. And the eleven they say aren't gold-bearing states, I can prove them wrong on at least half.

I pan and I teach people how to pan, but I also teach them how to use a sluice box. You can build them basically any size. You see pictures of these guys with a wooden box. It can be anywhere from a foot to eighteen inches wide, maybe thirty, forty, fifty feet long and they shovel into it and water runs through it. Well, water will wash the rest of the stuff away, but there are ripples in the middle that collect the gold. There's a lot of process here that people just really don't understand. When I teach gold mining, the first thing I teach people is that other than by man's hand gold never moves but by water. No animal goes and picks it up and takes it away because it's got no use for it. You can't eat it. I mean you could, but it wouldn't do you any good.

A while back there was a place like that I took my buddy, his wife, and two kids—a carnival up in Oregon. It cost like five dollars to pan. She wanted to learn how to pan. I said, "Why do you want to do it here, when I can take you out to a stream and do exactly the same thing and it ain't gonna cost nothin', and I've got all the pans and so on?" But she wanted to do it. When they handed me a pan it only had two ripples in it. I said, "I don't want this thing." "Well, what's the matter with that pan?" "See those pans up there that you sell people? Them pans are three ripples. I want one of them, because I want to teach her how to pan right." "Well, there's no difference." "Yes there is." I paid five bucks for her to pan, but she found probably ten to twenty dollars worth of gold, because she used a three-ripple pan. And that's what they didn't want, but they found somebody that knew what he was doing.

[On his recent travels.] I started to go up north. I got about Corning and the weather started turning bad. So I was going to head over to Arcadia. I've got a friend over there who's a glassblower and his wife makes jewelry. He wanted me to come up and do some panning so we could find some gold so he could incorporate it into his glassblowing and his wife's jewelry. I was waiting until about the middle of next month to go up into Oregon, because I've got a client coming out of Del Rio, Texas who wants to come over with his girlfriend and do some prospecting. She can only be gone for two weeks, but he owns three businesses, so he can take off whenever he wants. He wants to spend about a month or so.

The two best places for gold panning in the world, as far as I'm concerned, are Northern California and Oregon. There's a lot of difference in the gold. Elsewhere it's only about sixty, maybe seventy percent pure; whereas it's ninety to ninety-eight percent in Northern California and Oregon. There's a lot of difference in the gold. People don't know that. They think gold is gold and that's it. Hypothetically, if you were to take a gold nugget from Oregon or Northern California and you were to set it down next to gold from, oh, let's say Arizona or Alaska, within a week the one from Arizona or Alaska would be grayish-black all over, because of the silver content in it. It would tarnish real easy. Whereas gold that doesn't have all the other metals in it won't tarnish hardly at all. It's much better gold.

[I asked about him being a veteran.] I was in Vietnam '67, '68, and '69. I was one of those sent into Saigon for the '68 Tet Offensive. I was thirty-five miles out at a town called Phu Cuong with my outfit. About two o'clock in the morning they dropped helicopters in and said we're going into Saigon. They took us into Phu Tho Race Track, put a smoke screen around it, dropped us in the middle and said, "Kick ass coming out." We spent a month or better in Saigon in various sections of town chasing them back out of town. They came into town like they were going to a parade. Bold as brass they'd walk right down the street and kill anybody that was in their way. [Pause.] It was all about the almighty dollar. Johnson had Kennedy killed so that we could stay over there, because Johnson's wife owned a helicopter refurbishing company in Corpus Christi, Texas. I flew on a lot of helicopters when I was there and every time our helicopters flew for two hundred hours, they had to come back to the United States and be completely refurbished by her company. She also owned the ships that brought them back and forth and also the ships that brought us our supplies over there. Johnson didn't want us out of Vietnam and Kennedy was going to pull us out. They actually have recorded phone calls of him calling Kennedy's wife after, and he's trying to get in her pants. While I was in Nam I kept hearing things about him trying to pull us out, but he never tried to pull us out whatsoever. It wasn't Kennedy that put us in Nam; it was Eisenhower, but only as advisors. It was Johnson that actually escalated the war and kept it going. Nixon pulled us out. It was all about money, so is Iraq. I can agree with us being in Afghanistan looking for Bin Laden, but we're not even looking for Bin Laden. [Pause.] For two reasons: Saddam Hussein threatened Bush's dad when he was president. So it was a vendetta thing. The other thing is, Cheney, before he was vice president, was head of Halliburton. Who's the first company they send over there? The thing is, those companies are supposed to do bids. Halliburton never did bid, and they charge three times what anybody else would for the stuff that they did. There's numerous proof that Halliburton overcharges on a lot of stuff over there and nobody's ever done anything about it.

I listen to talk radio all the time. Certain people I like and certain people I don't. I can't stand Rush Limbaugh. He's a blowhard. He's a Democrat basher—that's all he is. And Shawn Hannity, he's the same way. I was listening to Hannity last night, and he's talking about how Obama's doing nothing right, that we're x-amount of trillions of dollars more in debt. Obama's trying to straighten out the shit that Bush and Cheney did. Give the man a chance, he's only been there a hundred days! He's done more in that hundred days than Bush did in his whole two terms.

Actually, I consider Clinton a damned good president in comparison. Bush is going to go down in history as being the worst president we ever had. There is no if, ands, or buts about it—he's an idiot. And now they're coming up with this stuff about Bush and Cheney allowing waterboarding. It's totally illegal and should never have been allowed. But you ask any of them, "No, no, it's perfectly fine; there's nothing wrong with it." Supposedly we're supposed to go by the Geneva Convention, which I agree with to an extent—"Nobody else goes by it; why should we?"

Me I'm pretty well versed on the law. I have beaten numerous cases. If I act as my own attorney, I'll beat it. If I allow somebody else to be my attorney, I'll wind up going to jail. If I handle it myself, I've beat almost everything I've ever come up against—unless I knew I was in the wrong. The worst thing I ever did? Both me and my wife got busted down in Florida for sixty-eight pounds of marijuana. It was all set up by her ex-boyfriend, because he though he needed her worse than me—and he was already married and had four kids. He accomplished exactly what it was he wanted to accomplish. While I was in prison, because I took the weight off of her, she divorced me.

I gave Mike a ride down to Los Angeles. He talked about picking up some money from a branch of his bank in Burbank where his VA check was being electronically deposited the next day.

Orange, California

Angel

Angel runs his own house-cleaning business along with his wife and cousin.

Business is bad, real bad. I've lost four customers just this week. Last year, at this time, I had twenty-five or thirty customers a week. Some I do once a month, some every week. Some customers didn't cancel but cut back from every week to once a month, then they cut back to zero for good, because they don't know what's going to happen. Some of my customers have their home business, and their business slowed down, so they have to cut me out. And others are on social security and they can't do it any more.

I think business is down about thirty-five percent for me. Usually we make about 400 [dollars per person], but last week we made about 320, 300. My first customer, the one I started with, she cut it off to once a month. They have their own business. Her husband does some service for cleaners. They had to finally lay me off. They tried hard for at least six months, then they said they can't afford it. I said, no problem. But you still have to pay taxes. [Laughs.]

So many people are starting to lose jobs. Before they were working and they needed somebody to clean houses. So many of the white people, the woman stayed home, because the man can afford to bring money to her, but not anymore. Not anymore.

My son, he was in the Army. He signed up for Orange County and LAPD. He's going to be twenty-one in August, but because so many people have been laid off and they've cut the departments, so he doesn't know if he'll get in.

I thought they gave veterans priority.

Not really. Not Really. He's only working part-time at night now. It's barely enough to make his car payment. He's still in the Army. He signed up for six years. He still has two. He went to Iraq. He told me if he doesn't get any job shortly, he wants to go to Kosovo. He'd get more money. It's not what they tell you in the beginning. They say you're going to get this, this, and that, but you're on your own. You're on your own. ■

Southern California

Orange, California

Carrie-Anne

Carrie-Anne is my niece on my sister's side. She is a Physician's Assistant in Southern California.

I have patients that have lost their jobs and are subsequently losing their insurance. The insurance cost $1,700 a month for them and their spouse and they can't afford it. And these are patients that need surgery or had surgery and now can't follow through with the therapy needed for their recovery. It's an instant loss of circumstances.

It's awful. Everybody's losing their homes. I think some people put themselves in a bad situation. People would buy and use their second mortgages and their third mortgages with the equity that they had in the home, then the housing market tanked and they owed $600,000 on this home that is worth $400,000, so now their screwed.

Oftentimes the banks are responsible for what has happened. They're the ones that lend the money. They're the ones that said, "Oh yeah, we can refi you. You have all this equity. Your house is worth $500,000. Sure we can give you that 200 grand you want for whatever." And now they want the home back, even though they're the ones responsible to begin with for lending the money.

My job's pretty secure, for now. I see health care abuse every day. We have a patient that has a knee problem they've had for twenty years, they trip and fall at work, then suddenly all their knee problems are because of that fall. You can tell the difference between a chronic tear and an acute tear. They're taking advantage of the system.

I have a friend who's been a teacher for ten years and she just got her pink slip. You don't want a bunch of stupid people roaming around; that's not really going to help the world. We need to educate out children. I mean, I had to go to traffic school recently. My first ticket ever. And in Orange County you're not allowed to go on-line—you have to go to traffic school! So I went to school for two Wednesdays for four hours and there are so many stupid people. They could not possibly have gone through our school system. It took an hour of explanation where to write their names on the form for the DMV. It was amazing. So, let's go out and take it away from education and make more of those people.

Some of it is greed. They make a lot of decisions that they think will benefit them now, but what about five years from now? It doesn't benefit anybody; it hurts everybody. Our situation today is that people that were planning on retiring, who had their money in 401Ks, trusted the system, they can no longer afford to retire. Can you imagine working your entire life planning for this day, then your retirement funds are now half of what they used to be. It's just awful. ■

Orange, California

Heather and J. Paul

Heather is Carrie-Anne's sister, my sister's firstborn, and my mother's first grandchild. J. Paul is her significant other.

Heather: If we were not together and I was on my own with my daughter and my current job I would be one paycheck away from…well, I'd already be behind. If I were to lose my job tomorrow…I don't have any savings. It's almost a joke when they say you should be saving. Really!? That twenty-five dollars or so a paycheck I'm supposed to be putting into savings is just not feasible. It's a co-pay at a doctor. I completely understand how people that lose their jobs and don't have a family support system can fall behind. I'm primarily in advertising and I don't feel all that secure in my job.

J. Paul: I'm in real estate. And I'm a mortgage broker. It's a double whammy.

Heather: My company's been through six rounds of layoffs. I've been fortunate. I know for a fact that when, or if, my cut comes it's not going to be because I don't do an awesome job. It comes down to money. Every day I go to work it's walking on eggshells.

J. Paul: Going back further than a year, I'd have to say it hit the mortgage industry first. There was a period in my industry, the mortgage broker industry, you could say pretty conservatively that it had been cut by fifty to sixty percent. It went down by more than half within a year. Mortgage values are still shot. People are still upside-down, but people that are fortunate enough to have equity and qualifying income can get great rates. Right around December, interest rates started plummeting and I was able to pull some more scraps off the table. I've been in commission sales for the last fifteen years. Ask me what my income's going to be next month and I don't know.

Heather: There're glimmers of hope. The head of my company goes around the country giving seminars to real estate agents and he always says, "Real estate got us into this mess and real estate's going to get us out." The indicators he sees are positive.

J. Paul: Banks are working with people now.

Heather: But they should have done it before. I worked in mortgaging myself for a while. Sub-prime lending, of course, and I was on the servicing side of these loans. It was a huge corporation—we had our own personal gym, we had our own personal cafeteria, Jay Leno came to our Christmas party. We were living the good life. But if there was anything outside that contract we did not work with people. Waiving pre-payment penalties, waiving a late fee—those things never happened. If you have any bad credit history at all you were punished. It wasn't like a case-by-case basis; it was a factory warehouse of loans. You're just a number. You're a FICO score. ■

Tustin, California

George

"Jorge" is married to a sister of my oldest friend. His is the great American success story. The son of Honduran immigrants, he has worked hard to get where he is with his insurance business. His world view is built on being honest, open, and hopeful. His family is riding out the rough economy fairly well. It hasn't been without its bumps, but as George says, "I feel blessed. I have my family and I have my health."

I live in Orange County, and it had an unemployment rate at one to three percent. You have pockets like Santa Ana where it was higher. You go to southern Orange County and they're doing really well. Even now, I doubt that the unemployment rate's any higher than six percent. [This was early May; four months later unemployment was at ten percent for the county as a whole.] You have pockets like that, where people have done well. As an insurance agent, I have 4,000 people and I hear all sorts of stories and I see the whole spectrum. I have an office in Newport Beach and I see people who are still doing really well and it hasn't really affected them, except maybe some of their investments have gone down. Some people were smart enough to avoid a lot of that and other people weren't. But the effect as to whether it's changed their lives or not—a lot of them it hasn't, but they'll call me and say, "I need to tighten up and cut expenses as much as possible. Is there anything in my insurance portfolio and my policies that I can trim?" Then I've got people in Riverside and the Inland Empire calling me who are losing their homes. I can tell when they're not paying their premium, and I follow up with them to find out that they're letting everything go and that the bank is repossessing it, so why pay the insurance? So there's a whole range. I hear their individual stories and it's tragic. So some people it doesn't affect; other people it affects emotionally. They're financially still where they were, but they're feeling vulnerable, because they're scared that they're living check to check. They still have their jobs, but they're not sure if their jobs are still going to be there. They might be the next wave of layoffs. I get that, because they're wanting to buy life insurance, for example, because they don't have any and they know that if something happens to them their family's going to be in a bad place; however, they don't want to commit to an extra forty or fifty dollars a month, because people have been laid off at work. I hear the range of stories. It ranges from people who've lost everything, to people who are financially still in the same place, but living with more fear, to those that have done well historically and are in a secure financial place, which is an interesting thing. The people who are still doing financially well are being affected to some degree in another area that has to do with a feeling of guilt—a survivor's guilt. I'm going to Europe, for example, and yet maybe I shouldn't go to Europe, because I'm spending all this money and people everywhere are hurting and maybe I shouldn't. I hear those stories. Anytime you have a historical downturn or near-depression it affects people in different ways.

For me, all of this makes me feel fortunate. I feel blessed. And I have for a long, long period of time, because I came out of poverty. My parents were born in Honduras, Central America. I came here in 1960 with my parents, having nothing. They moved here from Honduras because I had asthma really bad. I lived in a very humid climate and my parents were told to move to a dryer, more desert-like climate and I'd have less asthmatic reactions. My uncle lived here, so my parents followed. My dad had been a business owner in Honduras. He came here not speaking English. They took all their savings and moved here and my dad became a dishwasher and my mom cleaned houses as a maid. My dad had a second-grade education and my mom had a third-grade education, but they were hard working and they live the American Dream and all they wanted was their kids to have a better education and have an opportunity like everybody else. Eventually they bought a house in Santa Maria in central California. I went to school there, then I got a scholarship and went to UCSB and became a history major. After that I returned to Santa Maria and taught high school. From there I became an educational consultant and traveled all over the country. Later, I got married to Gayle...I met Gayle...well, I worked at Stanford University for two summers working with migrant kids. In Santa Maria you have a migrant population and I spoke Spanish. The reason I became a high school teacher was because I always wanted to travel and I wanted the summers off. Then I couldn't afford it, because I got married to my first wife and had a baby. So I would always teach in the summers. Then Prop. 13 passed and the funding was cut for school districts, and I lost my summer school job, but there was one program, the migrant education program and they were looking for model teachers, and I applied—I was actually sort of scouted. They hired me to work in this leadership-training program at Stanford. It was a novel education, radically different. I actually made a film. I was also going through a separation and divorce, and during that project I made the film. I also got selected to do a conference at the bilingual teacher's program and I showed this film. And Gayle came up to me at the end of this conference and unbeknownst to me she knew a teacher that worked at Stanford with me and that teacher had brought her to the conference for my presentation. So she came up to me and said that my movie was incredible and I was very touched. I asked where she was from. I tried to convince her to do the curriculum that I had done at Stanford. She was cute, so I asked her out. We dated for nine months, then got married. It was crazy. We met because of the work I was doing at Stanford. Eventually I left that school district and took a sabbatical and never went back to teaching, but I worked as a consultant with a training program in San Diego.

Politicians play games. And one of those games is the blame game. And clearly there have been abuses. And clearly some people who are in leadership positions in large corporations have been abusive, and they've hurt their shareholders. If people bought their stock on certain information and they were depending on dividends for their retirement—some of those business managers did not do a good job in terms of public trust. Small business owners have a trust, too—to their employees. For example, I have eight employees—even thought I don't have to, I provide medical and dental for them. I pay one hundred percent of everything. I could be pocketing that $40,000 a year. And there are lots of them who do that. It's my obligation—my moral obligation to do that. As an owner I have the ability to do that. This last year was the first time, in twenty-six years, that I've ever taken a decline in income. Yes, it's affected me. That negative was $100,000 down in income. It means less retirement money, but it didn't affect my lifestyle. The children are out of the house and off the payroll. That's why I say I was blessed. The timing was right.

I put three kids through college. Remember, I came out of poverty. I was the first one to graduate college in my family. It opened up my world—not only financially, but intellectually. I was a history major. I was exposed to stuff. If I hadn't had a college education, I would have felt I was deprived in some way. That was the one thing I felt I had to give my kids—and I was crazy about that—but I didn't want to make it my issue. For Gayle it was an important issue also. We sacrificed financially. My first daughter went to NYU and we were paying her tuition on credit cards. We went into debt. She got into NYU, which is a private school, and I was just starting my business career. It became easier for the other kids, but it was still a sacrifice. We paid almost $200,000 for my other daughter to go to Boston University, another private school, and I paid more than that for my son to go to George Washington University. It was the one thing I overindulged them in. They're intelligent; they've traveled the world. They feel blessed that they got the opportunity. Now they're all following their own dreams.

As a parent, that's the hard part, you have no control over their future. All you can do is be a good parent, be supportive and encouraging, and set limits. The reality is that all you can do is unconditionally love them, pray for them, and hope to give them the very best. And that's the hard part. That's the challenge.

Gayle and I feel that this downturn of $100,000 is perfect for us, because we've accomplished what we wanted to do. It's the golden opportunity of this country. The only thing in this country I believe in is hard work and education. If you have that drive; if you have that ability and you have the ability to get an education, then at least the doors are potentially open. You go through times like this, people are hardworking and educated, but there's no opportunity. When the country goes through a period like this, there are people who are willing to work—that's the sad part. There are just no opportunities.

That's the challenge for every human being in this country. It's been my motto that the real measure of a person is what you do with what you're given. If you're born poor in this country and you feel sorry for yourself—which is what I love about Barack Obama, by the way, is the fact that there's literally no excuse. You're given what you're given; you have what you have—whether you're given the most or very least. You just accept what you're given and make the very best of it. That's the true measure.

I had purchased two insurance agencies and combined them into my current agency, so I had taken a financial risk. I went into some major business debt. All of those were paid off. All my debts were paid off, except for my house. All my kids college education was paid off. So, the timing for me to lose this income was perfect. The only real issue was then, do I cut back on my staff, lay off people so that I can have more money for my retirement, or do I keep my staff and understand that eventually things are going to get better and that my income would come back up and then I wouldn't be left without quality people that I was committed to. I have good, hardworking employees that I've had for ten years. I felt responsible for them and for their livelihood and their families. I pay them very well and I give them great benefits. At my stage in life, that's what being an entrepreneur is to me—that I am adding to people's lives. I'm creating opportunities for them. If they're adding to my income, I have a measure of responsibility to them. It's part of my social contract that I believe in. This is an interesting period of time, because a lot of new people will take this as an opportunity to create new businesses.

Changing the way we tax would be the most radical and difficult thing to overcome. You have too many vested interests. There are CPAs, if you made it too simple everybody could do their own. You have tax attorneys, you have real estate agents…then there's collection. It's crazy. I don't know what the solution is. I just know that if you want it to be fair, it's not. The best example is that every time Obama wanted to get someone to work for him they had to fix their taxes.

Right now, if I sold my insurance agencies, would I have to pay it as a capital gain or would I have to pay it as ordinary income that gets taxed at a much higher rate. I've gone online and asked CPAs and I'm getting two different opinions. My point is that politicians, as a whole, don't have the will unless the American public demands that will to handle these difficult issues and really reform them—I think that's the big challenge. ■

Los Angeles, California

Los Angeles, California

Kevin and Amanda

I've know Kevin since high school. He lives in Los Angeles with his girlfriend, Amanda. He's worked for a California community college for—well, for a long time. Amanda is an art teacher.

Amanda: It's scary. We're doing okay. We both work at schools. We've been there a while. It makes the job difficult. My workload will increase next year. My classroom sizes are already pretty big. All the other teachers have roughly twenty students and now they'll have thirty-five. The dynamics of the school is changed. I've been hoarding supplies. Now I'm not going to use as many in the classroom and I'm going to stretch them out as long as they last. It was the first school that I'd been at that I didn't need to buy art supplies and finance field trips with my own money—all that is changing.

Kevin: My lack of ambition's finally paid off. It's just a regular job where you have to have at least one person doing it. I live in a cheap place. It's rent controlled. Our cars are paid off. They have a place down there [in his small bungalow complex]. I don't know what it actually looks like inside, but according to the *For Rent* sign out front, they want $1,800. But that sign's been out there for several months. There's an article in the paper today that buyers now are really trying to bargain. It's a great time to buy. People are finding that if they have a place, they're selling it cheaper.

Amanda: The bank takes over a home and then they sell those. They're still selling them for not that cheap. They're still trying to get their money. And then nobody can get a loan.

Kevin: (to Amanda) What are the houses like in Oklahoma?

Amanda: They're nice. They're not expensive, but they're not that cheap. They've built all these energy-efficient homes. There'll be neighborhoods where all the houses have the same floor plans. They're patio homes—not a lot of lawn. That's kind of a big movement.

Kevin: People used to come here because it was cheaper to live. Now they move out of the area because they can't afford it. A couple used to be able to get by on one income.

Amanda: All the women I knew, like my aunts, they worked. My mom didn't work, then she went into real estate when I was in junior high. She writes grants now. She's good at it. They throw out a lot of grants because they're not written correctly. They have all these rules. You have to have an idea and use statistics to explain why you need it. They really want somebody who can write things in the format. There's key words and proper language. I thought about taking classes. I have a friend who's a grant writer, but there's no money. There's no money for charities. That's another person we know who's hurting a lot. We recently lost our grant at my school. ▪

Las Vegas, Nevada

Janet and Sean

Janet and Sean are homeless in Las Vegas. I treated them to a modest breakfast and some conversation.

Sean: We're trying to get back on our feet. We trusted somebody and they screwed us. They were staying with us. They stole our stuff. Then they became vindictive, when we accused them, because they were the only other people in the place. So they went to the office and told them we were allowing them to stay there, which was against the rules. And we were kicked out.

Janet: Really good friends.

Sean: They weren't family, they were just somebody we thought we were helping. But it's not going to change us; it's not going to keep us from helping somebody. [To me.] We pray before we eat. [He proceeds with his prayer holding Janet's hand.]

Sean [Continued.]: I met Janet in Las Vegas after I got out of prison and I've been with her ever since.

You can't say you got out of prison and let it go at that.

Sean: Well the first time I was protecting a woman—

The first time?! It's just getting better.

Sean: —I was protecting a woman who was getting beat up by two guys. I brought a bat over there to protect her. They called it a weapon. The self-defense law in the state of Nevada is not recognized.

Janet: And they took that bat and beat him.

Sean: The second time, I yelled at my ex-girlfriend and it was verbal abuse. There was a cop behind me and they called it my third domestic and they sent me to prison—not jail, prison. I did one-to-four. They kept me in there until my full sentence was over. And I didn't get in *one* fight. They said they were going to use me as an example the first time. Hell, I was eighteen years old. I'm thirty now. [To Janet.] I'm her young tyke.

Janet: A puppy. [Laughs.] I'm from Chicago originally. I've been here eighteen years. My parents wanted to go where there was no snow. They were tired of the cold weather.

Sean: I was in Chicago one time. We were hitchhiking—an ex-girlfriend with a dog. The truckers would let the dog ride with us all around the country, everywhere. We stopped in Chicago and I went in there with a food stamp card, in this little convenience store. It had fifteen layers off glass, all bullet proof.

Janet: He was in a good part of town.

Sean: Friendly folk.

Janet: I used to work here—on the Strip—at the MGM.

Sean: Yeah. She used to be the pit crew supervisor for the MGM Grand. And because she gave everybody there… what was it?

Janet: Because, when I became supervisor, I kept things the way they were, the way the supervisor before me—my old supervisor—used to run things. As long as all the pits were caught up with their work, she'd let them take a break. If they weren't caught up, then they couldn't. Makes sense, right? Well, my manager didn't think so. She decided to get rid of me—after six years. She'd been in the casino business a lot longer than me. It's all politics along here on the Strip. Everybody knows everybody. Ever since then I've tried almost every casino. She's totally blacklisted me. They won't even give me a job as a cage clerk, let alone as a supervisor. That's the kind of person she is.

When they let me go, they gave me a choice. They said they were either going to terminate me, or I had to resign. And that's not a choice. If you resign, you keep your hire status with MGM Mirage. If they terminated me, I would have no rehire status and lose all my vacation time. So I had no choice; I resigned. I didn't think I was going to get my unemployment. I fought MGM. It took me six months to fight it. When we went to mediation, I was across the table from my old boss. She was going on and on, lying and lying. The mediator even said, "Everything you've said and all the evidence you've brought don't add up." She suspended me, then three and a half weeks later she terminated me. The mediator asked, "If what I'd done was so severe why didn't you terminate her the first time? Why did you wait three and a half weeks?" It's been almost three years and I've been out of work. I've worked with a temp agency. They'd send me out on a few assignments here and there, but that's been it.

Sean: My story is that I've been getting high almost my whole entire life. Speed. And I'm not straight yet. I'm not going to lie to you. I've tried, but when you're on the streets it's tough. People don't take you seriously. They look right through you. Right now I'm not high. It's been about [Looks at Janet.] nine days?

Janet: I don't get high as often now. I've been dying to put my feet up in a room.

Sean: We've just been camping out. We'll be all right in a couple of days. Her mom's going to send us some money. We're just kind of floating in the air. If we can come up with forty-six dollars and twelve cents we can stay at the El Cortez. I'll have to hide while she gets the room, because they'll charge you more. And we're not allowed at the Motel 6.

Janet: Once again, not our fault.

Sean: I offered to work for that one night. They told me to get fucked. Then they called the cops. [Pause.] Some guy fed us the other night. He asked why I didn't order steak. He was mad because I didn't order steak. But we didn't want to impose. So we ordered the special and he was angry. Angry.

Janet: Yeah. Steak was fine.

Sean: He wanted us to spend fifteen dollars each. But there's no way we can do that. We can't ask this individual...I can't accept that from somebody who works hard for their money. Not without working for it. I offered to shine his shoes and he said, "I'll shine your teeth with my shoes. You'd better order that steak." He was an older guy from Colorado.

Janet: Tell him about the surveillance. About licking the screen.

Sean: Oh yeah. I was playing one of the machines and losing my ass off. This was like a year and a half ago. I thought, well, if putting money in is not working, maybe I should just press max and lick the screen. And I was just joking. The next bet took a whole fucking dollar and I licked the screen and it went ding, ding, ding.

Janet: Seven out of seven on Kino.

Sean: I did it the next day, because I thought that it was going to happen again. I was going to show her...

Janet: Which machine it was and all that...

Sean: So I pressed max bet and I licked the screen and nothing happened. About fifteen minutes later five huge guys are standing by me. One of them said, "Patrol just said you licked that screen. Did you just lick that screen?" "Yeah, I licked the screen." "You guys are going to have to leave and never come back." Las Vegas is trying to defeat me and I'm not letting it.

Janet: He's a Leo.

Sean: I've got to perfect being in Las Vegas. If you can't make a dollar in Las Vegas, I've got a free hat I'll sell you. Eventually somebody will see that I'm a strong, hard-working guy. Who cares that I'm a convict? Which they look at a lot out here. They sift through a lot of California laws, but they enhance them out here. Everything. Domestic violence, because of O.J. in California.

Janet: Have you heard about any of our interesting laws here?

Sean: Like defacing a hamburger. Up to a year in the county jail. Impeding the flight of a pigeon. Flinching at it or squirting your car at it. Can be punishable by up to a year in the county jail. It's the state bird. [I looked it up. Actually, it's the Mountain Bluebird.]

Janet: And they enforce them.

Sean: Jaywalking is less offensive than attempted jaywalking. If you're going to jaywalk, then correct yourself by stepping off the curb and then stepping back on—that costs more money than actual jaywalking. And defacing a hamburger—this is how you deface a hamburger. You're standing next to a bum and you take your lettuce and tomato and you throw it on the ground. It's not against the law because it's biodegradable. But if you take it and throw in the trash or throw it on the ground in front of someone that's homeless and hungry, then *that's* defacing a hamburger. But if you feed the homeless in Nevada, that's against the law.

Janet: It's up to a thousand-dollar fine.

Sean: And there's that year in a county jail.

Janet: But I never, ever heard of feeding somebody…

Sean: When Oscar Goodman [Mayor of Las Vegas] first said that, I don't know how many state officials went out and fed the homeless.

Janet: They were having festivals.

Sean: It's manslaughter to drive over or pull out any—what kind of cactus is it?

Janet: Saguaro? There are people serving sentences.

Sean: It's horrible out here. But at the same time, there's a lot of Christians, Catholics, Mormons…

Janet: A lot of Mormons.

Sean: A lot more Mormons. [Pause.] We're Christian. ▪

Hoover Dam — Lake Mead, Nevada

Barringer Crater Enterprises complex — Arizona

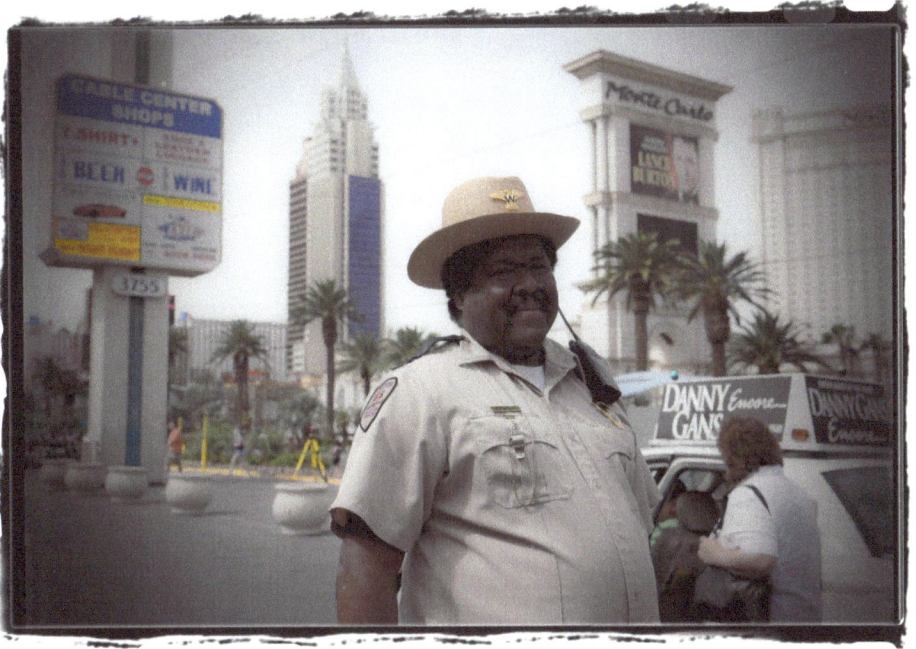

Las Vegas, Nevada

Willie

Willie is a security officer for several small properties along the Las Vegas Strip. There used to be four who patrolled the area during the week; that's been cut to two.

I've been doing security for seven years and I've been in Las Vegas about five. In 2000 I retired from the military and I went back home to Los Angeles. Things were expensive there. During that time the houses were still cheap here, so that's why we came out here. I bought a house; the value went up, then it took a dive. I've been here ever since. I retired from the Navy, but I've still got a sixteen-year-old—one more kid at home.

The economy's affected Las Vegas, but not that much. I still see people coming here. I have another part-time job as a limo driver. I'm still seeing companies sending people here; they're sending their clients to high-end hotels. I noticed a slowdown when the President mentioned the companies spending the bailout money. I noticed a slowdown here, but it only slowed down for a week, then it picked back up.

There were a few projects that were cancelled like the—not cancelled, but on hold—like where the old Stardust was. That building went up to the fifth floor and stopped. Now all they have is security guards watching it. And City Center [across the street], a lot of other countries have it. It's designed for you to live there. There's supposed to be doctor's offices, Walmarts, schools… Everything's supposed to be green and environmentally friendly. It's designed for you to live there and never have to leave.

The economy's affected me a little bit, because a lot of the security clients are canceling or cutting back. But business here on the Strip, they can't survive without us. They need us here, but there's other places that I've worked that they're cutting back so much. I still drive limo and they don't cut back, because you're on one hundred percent commission. I notice when people stop coming. I notice the trend at the airport. The lines and the flights that used to come in—it's not as much as before.

I think the economy's going to take a little bit longer than six months to go back up—maybe a year. A lot of guys are saying they predicted that the housing market was going to crash. I predicted that! I could see they were getting too expensive too quick. Like I said, I predicted that it would crash and it pretty much did here.

[About President Obama.] A hundred days, that's not enough. It takes years and years. I don't think it matters if he got in or it was the next guy. It's almost to a point that there's nothing to do, but get better. ■

Somewhere — New Mexico

New Mexico

Somewhere Else — Texas

Dairy Queen — Texas

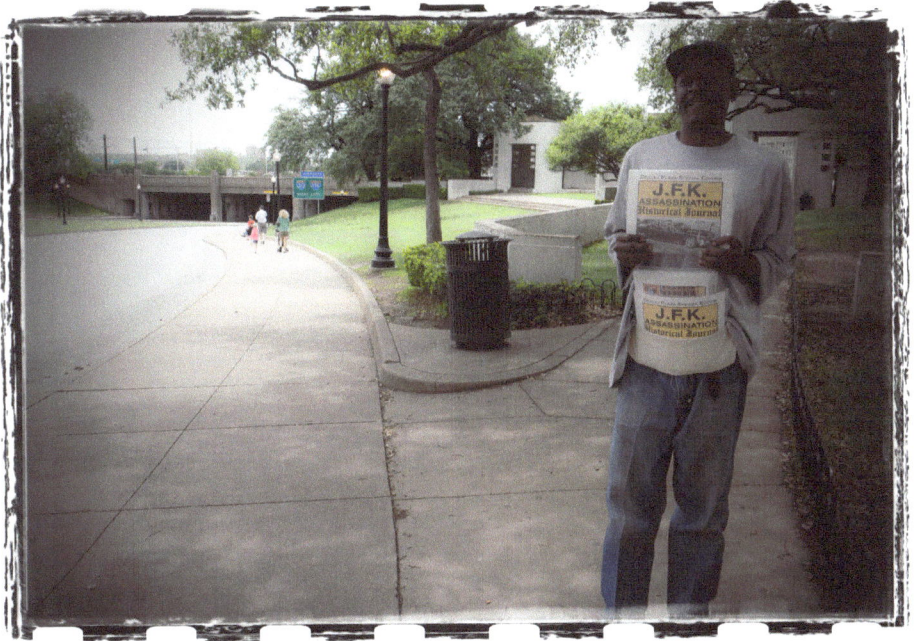

Dallas, Texas

Scott

Scott has been telling people about President Kennedy's assassination for the past seventeen years. He was two-years old when it happened. Behind him lies the site of that terrible deed and the infamous grassy knoll.

The assassination of JFK, I did believe at first was a conspiracy, then about seven or eight years ago I believed Oswald did it, but then I came back to my senses and believe it was a conspiracy. I believe there was other shooters at the grassy knoll. He [Kennedy] came from Main Street. It would have been a better shot. See, there's one part of me—from my years of being here—there were people that come to say Oswald was the only gunman. And they'd explain it to me, but then I come back to my senses when people came from the other group and said they believed shots came from the grassy knoll. They told me a lot of information why Oswald could not be the only gunman to do that, because of the situation of the assassination itself.

The economy has really taken a big toll on the…I'm going to tell you: Dallas is a pretty smooth-running city. But yes, the economy here has taken a big toll on the tourists. We're not getting a lot of them. It's very slow. We're probably down. I'm pretty good though.

I was born and raised with President Ford. I'm a Michigander. All my people are in Michigan. Their economy is like…[gestures thumb down]. I haven't been there in thirty years. I called my mother yesterday for Mother's Day. I told her I'm doing great. But the economy there is very bad. There are no jobs. GM is closing up. It's real bad. But in Texas we are moving along just pretty good. I think this is one of the most intelligent and richest states in America. No homeless. It's very clean here. A lot of rich people, too. ■

Dallas, Texas

Ralph

Ralph has owned and operated the Hollywood 5&Dime (his spelling) for fifteen years. It's located directly across from the Texas State Fairgrounds (home to the Cotton Bowl). He caters to a fifties/retro clientele. I met with him in the late afternoon and I was only the second customer of the day. Most of the businesses on either side of his have closed their doors. Some weeks he makes just fifty dollars and he may be out of business by the time this book comes out.

I had a bunch of friends in L.A. I had a store in Hollywood for a while. Someone was kind enough to break in and set my store on fire. So that's why I ended up back here. It's a snake pit out there. I was just lucky I had a bunch of friends out there from Texas and I'd lived in London for a while and friends from there moved to L.A.. I consider myself lucky in that respect, that I didn't stay out there longer.

I've had this store fifteen years. Yeah, I had another store in the neighborhood around the corner here from about '86 to '93 as well. I came here in '94. They kind of ran me out of business around the corner and they're trying to do it again. They're just now getting all this stuff straightened out. [About extensive roadwork in front of his store.] They've had the roads blocked off. I've heard the rumors about redevelopment, but they keep renting spaces. That building right there has a plaque on it from 1907 and it might be historical, but this particular building, I don't know. I've been here a long time myself, but there're tons of people that know more about the area than I do.

9/11 was bad for business, but last year about the first of June, gas went to four dollars a gallon and it pulled the rug out from underneath me. That's when these other businesses went away. [Note: All the small businesses on either side of his shop are closed.] The Bar of Soap lasted until Labor Day—and it had been there for twenty years. This place [Directly next door.] went about July or August. And I said, what the hell's going on. That's when my numbers…I mean, I've lost a thousand dollars a month basically for the last year, now that it's coming up June again. I feel lucky to be here. I figure I'll probably close this coming January. I've been able to sputter along on a little bit because I print t-shirts, too. That's been able to help me along. I do other shops and a few bands.

I had some friends that printed some shirts for the O.U. games over there [The Oklahoma Sooners play football across the street at the fairgrounds.] and the guys came around and confiscated their stuff. Oh, they'll do anything to keep the little man from making any money. And then gas went back down, but it really hasn't changed. I really can't tell. It hasn't come back like it was before. So, like I said, I feel lucky to be here this long, just because from June last year I was trying to hang in here until Christmas—and the Christmas really didn't happen. January's always real slow anyway, so I figure I'll probably be closed in January or February.

There used to be a nightlife scene here. There were restaurants that'd stay open 'til three in the morning. I'm not really down here at night. I close at eight o'clock. I could make more money if I was, but I kind of have a personal life. I can't spend my whole life down here. I guess I should if I had any sense. I could be making money. And that's another part of my problem. I've never made a living off of these other businesses, but now that there're none down here, there's no traffic—period. Over the years, I've had people come in and say we were at the bar last night and we saw your shop and wanted to come check it out. Now there's just no activity.

I began wondering, like in July of last year, what's the deal? I can go for days and not even see anybody. There's been like fifty-dollar weeks. It's supposed to be open in September. [About the new transit station being worked on between his store and the fair grounds.] The fair starts at the end of September and that's when they're supposed to have it open. I hope to hold out. I do my little British bike events down here, a little rally I hold at my shop. I do one Memorial Day, which is coming up, and then I do another one at the end of summer on Labor Day. So I'm hoping to hang in here for that time, anyway. We'll see. I've just been selling off some of my guitars and musical equipment. I never planned on being buried with the stuff, but I thought I might upgrade. I've got four cars and two motorcycles; I really need to unload some of that stuff, too. I've got a '56 Chrysler Imperial, a '58 Buick Riviera as well, a little '66 Chevy panel truck… I bought that Imperial about twenty years ago, and there're just no Chrysler people down here. There're some out West, for sure. I know guys around San Francisco that are big Mopar [A parts manufacturer for Chrysler, Jeep, and Dodge.] guys, but back East and up North, Chrysler's a big deal. But around here, man, I've never found anything for my car. It doesn't really need anything, but I'd hoped to find factory floor mats. I'd carried a list for ten years to swap meets. I've never bought one thing off that list. ■

Greater Dallas Area, Texas

Truck fire — Interstate 40, Arkansas

Hot Springs, Arkansas

William J. Clinton Presidential Center — Little Rock, Arkansas

Nashville, Tennessee

Robin

Robin is a street musician in Nashville. The box between him and the guitar case is filled with kittens (Nashville Cats), that he was attempting to give away in between songs.

Once, Alice Cooper was in town and heard Robin performing, "I'm Eighteen." Mr. Cooper told him he liked his version and proceeded to sing the song with him. What a moment. Sorry to say, there's no video.

I'm originally from Port Arthur, Texas. I've been here for about nine years. I'm retired military. And I've been playing on the street for about six years.

Tourism is cut back. Tipping is cut back because of the economy. A lot of my friends live in motels and they have to pay weekly or monthly rates, so they have to work longer hours just to get by. Luckily, I have a military pension, otherwise I'd be in trouble. From what I see, it's pretty rough now. ◼

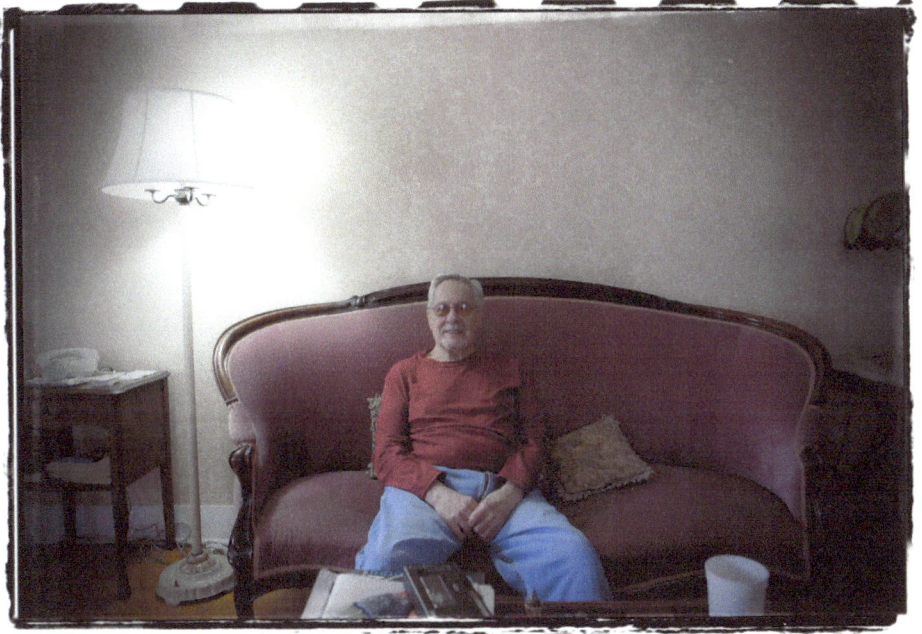

Knoxville, Tennessee

Bill

Bill is the cousin of a good friend and a retired music professor from the University of Tennessee at Knoxville. He still lives near campus with his wife in the home they bought in 1975.

The economy's not been really bad until lately. It was late hitting here. Local businesses did not close down, but in the last year there's been a significant rise in unemployment. I'm not sure why it hit later here. We have a saying though, "I want to be in Knoxville when the end comes, because Knoxville's always twenty-five years behind."

I retired in '94 from UT after teaching thirty-seven years there. Part of my retirement was with TIAA-CREF and just last month I got a notice that I'm being cut about $6,000 on their investment in stocks, so it's gone down there. I play in the Knoxville Jazz Orchestra, and as musicians we've taken a hit, too. A lot of people have cut back on their hiring for weddings and parties. I still get paid the same when I get a gig though. There's just less of them. And there're less players in the band. There's a piano player, he was actually a saxophone major, but he's a great piano player. He and I do a lot of duo things. We joke about it when we get to hire a drummer with us. We call that a big band gig.

This town is in the middle of poverty. When I first moved here in '57 I ran into a drummer I'd played with and he asked me if I knew where I'd moved to. Yeah, Knoxville. He said it's the bowels of Appalachia. We're just sixty miles from Kentucky and coal mines. We really are on the edge of Appalachia. It's a relatively poor town, so a lot of the architecture is not pretty. Some of it's nice. You should go downtown and take a look.

My Social Security actually went up a little. When I retired, they gave me some money from the university—they paid me to get out. I found out that between being able to draw Social Security and keeping the TIAA-CREF retirement and playing gigs that I could make about as much, if not more, as staying at the school. I was ready to quit anyway.

The CREF-thing and the shortage of gigs are the only things I've taken financial hits on.

I kid the guys about opening an apple stand with a little white lightning down underneath for needy customers. But it's nothing like the Great Depression. I lived through that. I was born in 1929, so I grew up in the thirties seeing all that. ◼

Dixie Caverns — Salem, Virginia

Alice, Michael, Michelle, and Thomas

We met on a tour of Dixie Caverns in southwest Virginia. There was nothing about the good-natured quartet that hinted at the profound loss and heartache they had experienced as a family. No photo.

I e-mailed Alice for any clarifications and corrections, since I had summarized our conversation from notes, not a recording. The core of her response can be found on page 107.

Michelle is Alice and Michael's niece. Thomas is Michelle's husband. In her thirties, Michelle had recently made a major career change from photography to law enforcement. A few months earlier, after graduating from the academy, she'd joined a nearby police force. As she showed me her badge, I asked what prompted her to become a police officer. Alice spoke up and said, "Because our daughter was murdered a few years ago."

Needless to say this became the story.

The men remained largely silent as Alice cathartically recounted her daughter's life and death and the aftermath. As she told me how Allison had died being a good Samaritan, she reached into her purse and pulled a photograph from her wallet. Allison was a beautiful young woman. She was twenty-three when she died in 2003. She left behind a husband and a young son.

The short version of Allison's murder is that she was working in a dual-use warehouse complex as a secretary at a construction business office. She heard screaming outside in the hallway and opened the door. A bloodied, shirtless man stumbled into the office. As she was attempting to render assistance, a second man entered the office and stabbed both of them to death. The assailant was later caught, tried, found guilty, and is now fighting his death sentence in the Florida Supreme Court.

Alice candidly told me of the deep depression she fell into at that time. She'd lost a son a few years before to an automobile accident. She showed me his photo. It all seemed like too much for one person to bear. But her niece, Michelle, would phone her every day to check in on her. She'd ask if she wanted to do something—to go out. She never gave up. Everyday Michelle would pester Alice to the point that Alice grew angry. Smiling now, she looked at Michelle, and said she was glad she didn't give up.

Somewhere in all this, Alice's sister, Michelle's mother, died. The bond grew exponentially between aunt and niece. They swore they weren't going to see their relationship as a mother-daughter substitute, but that's how it's evolved.

I have to admit to being in mild shock at the time. The terrible nexus of events these people had experienced and the amazing grace, courage, and strength they displayed left me feeling humbled and inspired.

My apologies to Michael and Thomas. I know their loss is great, too. But I was so taken by Alice and Michelle's positive dynamics, that I neglected to explore their stories. ■

Allison's son (Hunter) was just shy of three-years old when Allison was murdered.

Unfortunately, (for us) the murderer won his appeal for a new trial in the Florida Supreme Court. The Prosecutor has since submitted the case to the United States Supreme Court for it to overrule the Florida Supreme Court's decision. So, again we have to wait. The case won't be heard until 2010.

My son (Christopher) died in 1989 along with his girlfriend in an automobile accident. Both were 16-years old. He and Michelle were more like best friends growing up than cousins. They were only a year apart in age. Michelle took his death very hard. Michelle named her children after them.

Michelle's mom (Rose Marie) died after Chris in 1993 from cancer. Rose was also Chris' godmother.

Allison was murdered September 24, 2003.

Something that was not said when we met, but that you might have noticed, was how proud we are of Michelle and the decision she made to go into law enforcement. It is very unusual for an older, smaller-sized female to endure and succeed in the rigors needed to get into a law enforcement agency as she did. She has a photo of Allison posted in her patrol car.

National Museum of the Marine Corps — Quantico, Virginia

Rolling Thunder — Washington, D.C.

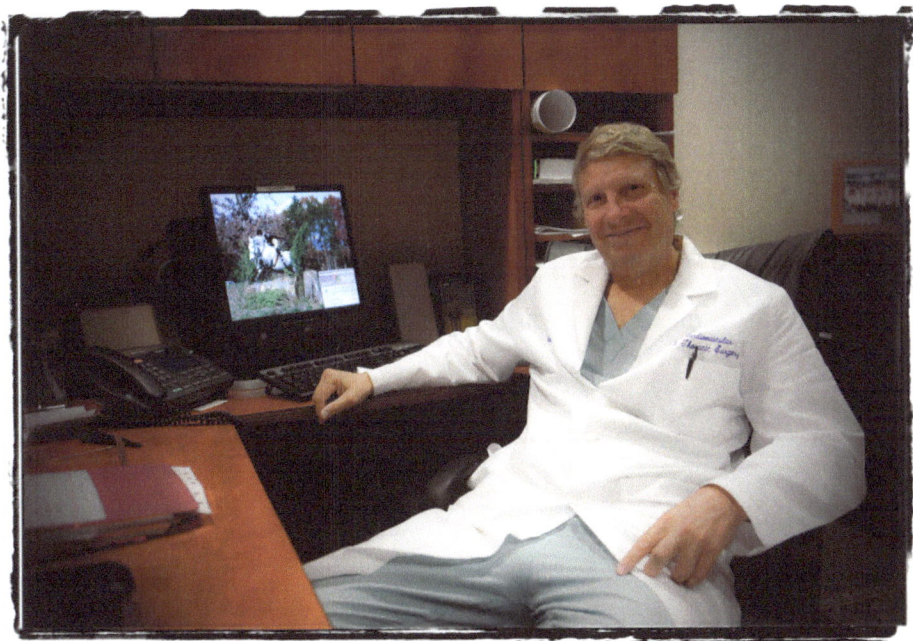

Falls Church, Virginia

Alan

Alan is the Medical Director of Cardiac Surgery Services for a major hospital just south of Washington, D.C. and a renowned cardiac surgeon. He's been there since 1982. That's his wife making a winning equestrian jump on the screensaver.

Like everybody else, the savings have fallen, the style of living is degraded. We have all reassessed retirement. Many of the physicians in my specialty have left the specialty. In our residency slots, for the sixth year in a row, only half are filling—so the demand for appropriate technicians is going to be a real issue for health care delivery in cardiovascular disease, because of absent cardiovascular surgeons. One of the primary reasons is the reimbursements have been cut almost eighty percent since 1995. You couple that with length of training, malpractice costs, standard of living—those guys work about eighty hours a week. Add to it a precipitous decrease in reimbursement, with another twenty percent cut, people say, "Why bother. I'm not going to do it."

The economy both for the longer term and the shorter term has really impacted on our ability to practice. And then, secondarily, so many of the patients have put off accessing care, because they don't have the funds. They've lost their insurance. They can't afford their medication. So by the time we're seeing them, they are quite ill. And the cardiologist is doing a yeoman's job to be supportive, but again, to what end?

I think in terms of access to primary care and internal medicine, it's dismal, and it will be unavailable. We can't get an internist to see our patients, because they are so busy. So, if we have an unassigned patient that comes in and we get them from the airport, that are *in extremis,* that need medical follow-up, there's nobody to send them to, because the internists don't have the time and they're totally filled. Most of the internists, the reimbursement is so bad, they simply don't accept insurance any more. Patients subscribe [to a doctor's services as an alternative], paying a certain amount a year to go to a particular doctor. Now, of course, the government is stepping in, saying that these individuals are practicing insurance and they want to stop it.

It is a mess. And it's going to be a worse mess. Our health system is in a great fall. But paying the doctors isn't the issue, in my estimation. You have these huge insurers with multiple layers of infrastructure, but the easiest thing to do is go straight to the physician reimbursement as the source of the problem. People are just going to say, We're not going to take care of them. So it's pitting the doctors against the patients, ultimately. The Medicare reimbursement is so bad that the physician can't stay in the practice. They're getting five to seven dollars an office visit. When I see a follow-up for a complex problem, it's twelve dollars.

Alan asked me what I thought the average reimbursement amount for cardiac triple-bypass surgery was (four hours operation time and thirty days of follow-up care). I had no idea. I made two wild guesses from high to low—and I was still not low enough.

It's nine hundred dollars.

The public perception is that there's this exorbitant fee that physicians are charging. It takes us probably four hours and attorneys are charging five hundred an hour. Those leaving the profession are becoming chief medical officers or health care administrators or going back and getting some other business degree or getting out of health care *in toto.*

I think you're always going to have to have an intermediary. You probably have to address the uninsured and the indigent—that's a huge problem. Medicare fraud is more and more of a real issue. Another issue insurers and politicians never really talk about is access to care and our unrealistic expectations of technology. As we're all now aging and we've got people in their eighties, should everybody have dialysis? Should all of them have open-heart surgery? Should all of them have all of these tertiary care modalities? Most other countries have solved that by saying, if you can't pay for it, then when you're over some age you don't get dialysis…and it does limit it, but it's not this endless free-fall with our elderly, where they get kidney transplants to gain a few months to a year. But that is such an ethical hot potato that it's total chaos to bring it up, so they leave it to us. Then what happens is it becomes more and more about public access—what is my outcome? If you're operating on somebody in their middle age, their expected mortality is about one percent. If they're an octogenarian, certainly in their nineties, their stroke rate is going to be ten percent and their mortality five percent. So, if it's published, it's going to be this is his coronary bypass results; this is his aortic valve replacement results. The hope is that because of that external scrutiny, we will limit for ourselves who we will operate on. It's not working.

There's got be some very real expectations of a federal plan. It's absolute. There's got to be some reimbursement for the uninsured. And there's also got to be some tort reform relief from the frivolous lawsuits. Just because I'm named, I can be dropped from my insurer—regardless of the validity of the suit. It costs an average of $35,000 just to defend. Most of the insurers say, "Just pay the $35,000." It's quicker to do it. But once that goes against me, then I can't get insurance. So, you've got neurosurgeons and orthopedists leaving the bigger cities because of this issue.

I have some real concerns. My son just graduated from George Washington University. He was on an Army scholarship. He owes them six years of active service. The average debt of these young people is $250,000. And when they pay it back it's $500,000. So how are they going to afford that? First of all, that may dictate what specialty they go in. Secondly, most of the people won't pick up that debt. So they'll say, We're not going into that specialty, because again, why stay up all night and work the weekends? It precludes ever buying a house or ever starting a family. So, there's no quick answer. Trying to help folks with tuition reimbursement, particularly dependent on which specialty they go in. We have a shortage of primary care physicians, should their tuition be supported someway? I'm not advocating that there's no malpractice—there is. They should be resoundingly criticized and prosecuted. Conversely, there has to be some forum where the guys that are really working hard, that their malpractice premiums aren't out of control and not dropped. In terms of reimbursement, a lot of this has to be taken into account as well and we have to decide: Are we going to take care of everybody? Or some of the people? It's not going to be income derived. There's got to be some middle ground where people don't suffer for that. It's a tragic time. People can't keep their lights on. One hundred percent of these practices are small businesses with one or two people in a very thin veneer of support. ■

Daniel

I talked with Amish proprietor, Daniel. Along with his family, he provides fresh produce, baked goods, flowers, and more at his open-air stall in Harve de Grace, Maryland (Unique on the Chesapeake). He would not allow me to take a portrait-like photograph of him, but I was free to catch him helping customers. I also couldn't record him. The flower portion of his business is down slightly, but his produce section is selling more. He, like others, thinks this is due to people staying closer to home for trips and vacations. The strawberries looked exceptionally good. I bought some homemade root beer before I left. I really enjoyed the high-energy kid in the (now deleted) photo. He thought Daniel was a hillbilly, which made Daniel laugh. ■

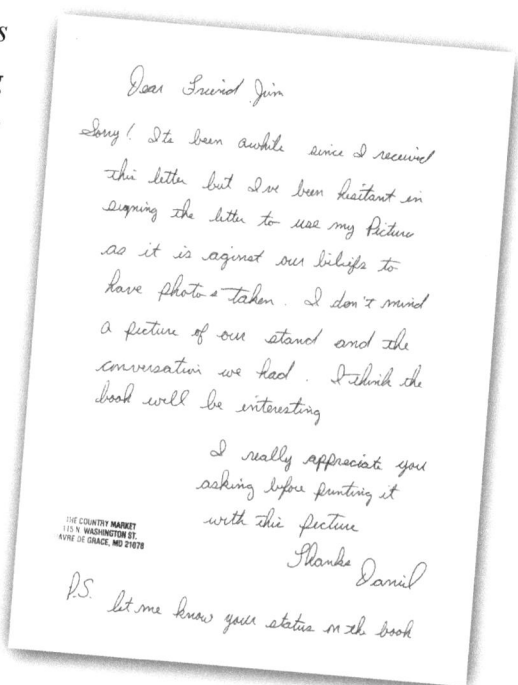

Dear Friend Jim

Sorry! It's been awhile since I received this letter but I've been hesitant in signing the letter to use my Picture as it is against our beliefs to have photos taken. I don't mind a picture of our stand and the conversation we had. I think the book will be interesting

I really appreciate you asking before printing it with this picture

Thanks Daniel

THE COUNTRY MARKET
115 N. WASHINGTON ST.
HAVRE DE GRACE, MD 21078

P.S. let me know your status on the book

I'd failed to secure a photo/interview release from Daniel when I was in Maryland, so I mailed him one at his Country Market address. At the eleventh hour, just before this book went to press, I received a letter back from Daniel requesting removal of his photograph. I had also neglected to take any photos of just his stand without him or his children in it.

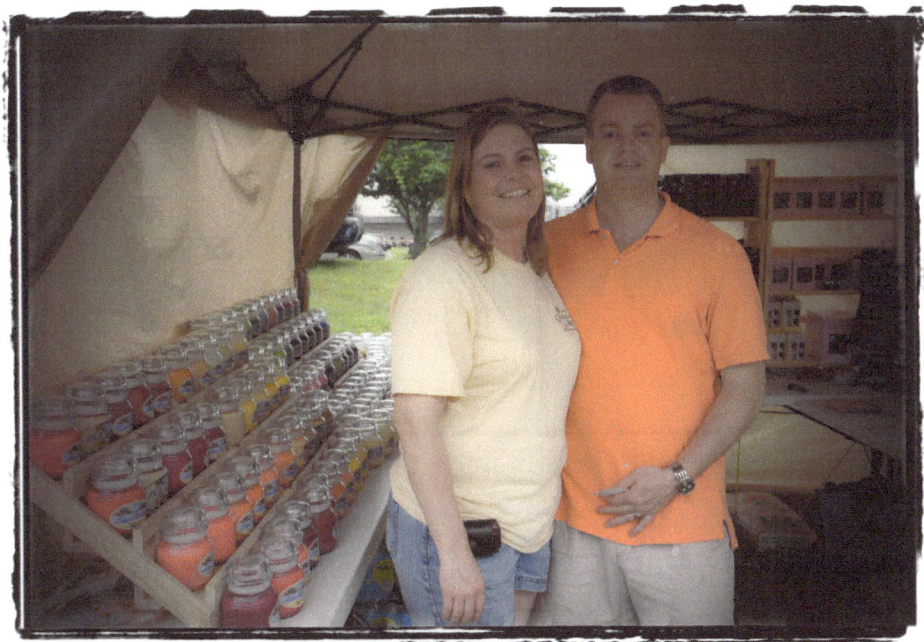

Dover, Delaware

Toni and David

Toni and David were out selling candles, soaps, and fragrances at a NASCAR event in Dover, Delaware. They seemed very upbeat about their corner of the economy. Their business card reads: "Fragrances, Fund-raisers, Opportunity!"

David: We sell an all-natural wax candle with one hundred percent cotton wicks. It's virtually a silt-free candle. It's a much better candle than you'll find at your dollar stores or supermarkets. We have an all-natural hand soap, a hand cream and foot cream developed by clinical dermatologists. We mostly do the crafts shows, but we are NASCAR fans. We're doing the race here in Dover, because we live just six miles away.

Toni: Because this is a multi-level marketing company that we do this for, we have our offline coming in tonight, so they'll be with us tomorrow and part of Sunday also. And our downline is actually coming in on Sunday and we're taking them to the race. So we'll see the race. We have plenty of help.

David: We believe the down economy is actually helping us. It's a consumable product that mostly women buy and we're experiencing that when they can't go out and pamper themselves to the degree that they want. There's a bottom line that they say, I can't do a day spa, I may not be able to get a pedicure, but you know what? I'm going to reach in my purse and get that twenty dollars and I'm going to get that candle.

Toni: It's a lifestyle item. There are certain things that women are not going to give up. Makeup's one of them. Scented candles. It's not like they're going out and buying a car; you're buying a candle. It's something that makes them feel good right now. And in an economy like this, it's something they're going to buy. They're getting a good product.

David: Again, it's multi-level marketing, and we have an on-line website where you can purchase all the products. Mostly the on-line business is recruiting. There are people above us and there are people below us, but we are partners in this business.

Toni: The people below us can go out any given day and make more money than we do. It depends. It's funny, because at some of the craft shows we've been at we had candles flying off the shelves and the person next to us would just pack up the bus, because they hadn't sold anything. It depends on what it is. Jewelry's non-consumable; you can only buy so much.

My husband, David, is going to be retiring from the Air Force in a few years. Our dream is to sell our home, get an RV, and go race to race. And this is something we could do while we're at the races. Right now we have this big beautiful home and we don't even use it. We like to go out to places, so what the point of having the home? The dog gets more use out of it than we do. ■

Closed Circuit City, Delaware

Dover, Delaware

Bruce and Art

Bruce and Art are brothers—one lives in Florida and the other in New Jersey. They shared a beer with me as they joked about their last name. That's the Dover International Speedway (The Monster Mile) in the background.

Bruce: I work for a freight company, ground and warehousing. The volumes are down. People aren't spending. So we've seen the volumes go down depending on the region—maybe over thirty-five percent, and in some places forty.

Art: I'm between jobs right now. It wasn't because of the downturn. I left one place and…well, it wasn't figured on. I'm just between jobs.

Bruce: I still have a job and I'm a happy guy. Our company was hit pretty hard. They clipped about twenty percent of the company from top to bottom at all levels across the board. There were some pay considerations made at certain levels. We're taking a beating.

We're contract freight. If you need something moved—if you're a manufacturer or some other industry, like refrigerators or computers— you have to get your stuff to market. We transport it. And we're impacted worldwide. The U.S. is the worst, but other segments of our business have been affected.

Recently I was at a meeting where a financial analyst was saying the economy's still dropping, but it's starting to taper off. It's got to the point where you're out of business or you're bare bones.

Art: The Circuit City's are open one day, then the next they're all locked up.

Bruce: Everybody's worried. There's not one person I talk to that hasn't said something—I don't know what to do. I hope it doesn't get any worse. ■

Howard Dean and union members — Elsmere, Delaware

Howard Dean

I stopped in to hear former Vermont governor, U.S. presidential candidate, and chairman of the Democratic National Committee, Dr. Howard Dean, speak about health care at the Sheet Metal Workers' Hall in Elsmere, Delaware.

Note: This is my one exception to not using last names, since Howard Dean is such a prominent figure.

The union hall was slow to fill, which pushed Howard Dean's arrival back more than half an hour. There were many politicos in attendance. Finally things started off with a woman speaking about the Employees Free Choice Act. Then a state representative warmed up the crowd by praising Dean's efforts to help reform health care. The microphone was handed over to a woman who related her health care horror story. Finally Dr. Dean took the stage. He was gracious to the union members, then dove into the reasons for a nationalized health care system. He's a good soldier in getting President Obama's message out there. And he knows how to play a crowd. Fun to watch. He eventually turned it over to questions and answers. Many expressed their concerns for health care reform. I left before the rush. ∎

Philadelphia, Pennsylvania

Brian

Brian drives a horse-drawn carriage around historic Philadelphia, giving tours. He's been doing it for sixteen years. Truman is his horse.

I started in February of '93. It's seasonal, but I work all year round. It's feast or famine. It really is.

Truman's about nine years old, the best I can tell. A draft horse lives thirty to thirty-five years. He'll work about another ten and then he'll be retired. I work for a company, it's owned by my two brothers. Before this I worked in theater out in Hagerstown, Maryland for six years as assistant technical director. And I was the assistant stage manager for the Maryland Symphony Orchestra. I spent another six years in New Bedford, Massachusetts where I worked for a theater, too. I'm working here because my family had horses when I was a kid over in the River District, Port Richmond. I worked at my Uncle Charlie's stable back in the sixties. My first job was mucking stalls in 1968. He was the one who gave me the fundamentals on driving a horse, rather than riding it. He had an old Ford wagon and an old mare and he took me down these old roads and showed me the basics. Later on, when I was looking for work, when I was coming back from Massachusetts, he had passed on, but his wife was still alive, and she told me my cousin had started one of these companies. By the time I came back it had been sold. She made a call to the new owners and recommended me to the new owner of the company. I have the horse experience and I have the know-how to operate around vehicles—and do it safely, defensively. I'm licensed by the city.

We don't get paid a salary. We get paid by commission and tips. That's why I was telling you, it's feast or famine. If I don't get a ride any particular day, I don't get paid. So it's really to my benefit that I hone my skills. There's no union, but I started the Association of Philadelphia Tourguides (APT). We were founded in August of '08 in response to the city's proposed ordinance that we have to take a history test. I thought it was kind of silly. I'm already doing this sixteen years, now you're going to tell me how to do my job. There're also some constitutional issues along with that as well. [And this in the shadow of Independence Hall.] It's my first human right. Am I supposed to force-feed you a history tour? Every ride is a custom ride, because I never know who I'm talking to or what they're interested in. Another constitutional issue is equal protection under the law. And the way the ordinance is written, not all tour guides in the city will have to take this test. Some will be exempt. It's pending.

One of the founders of the APT is involved with a federal lawsuit right now over at the 4th District Court, across from where I picked you up, and they're going on the constitutional issues. The judge can see it. He's trying to give the city enough time to correct their response, to modify the ordinance—namely, the one that provides exemptions. Being an amateur historian, I understand why they want it. In any city you're going to get folklore and myths, but when you decide to open you mouth about history, you'd better do just that. But you don't really know, unless you were there, what really happened. For instance, Betsy Ross. There's no documentation that she sewed America's first flag. She sewed the Pennsylvania Navy's battle ensign. We know that. But in 1876, when the Centennial celebration took place in our city, Alexander Graham Bell was here with his telephone. Everything in the city was really happening. It was like a World's Fair. Betsy Ross' grandson started to put this story out about his grandmother making this flag. Rightly thinking that she does deserve some historical credit. Anyway, some of the tour guides here are dispensing incorrect information or just half-baked ideas.

The judge tried to put a six-month injunction on the proposed ordinance, because he wants to consider it. He's given the city an opportunity to modify their position. It's just silly. They told the judge, to mollify him, that they just wanted to enact it and we're not going to enforce it. What are you going to do? Have history police? We're interpreters. I interpret history. What I've done is crosschecked it at least once if not more. The ride can be more theater than history lesson. It depends what the customer wants. If somebody wants straight history, I'll do that. I always try to interject a little humor and I always try to correct misconceptions. If somebody says something that's not true, I don't let them walk away from me. At least, they should hear a different version.

With this gentleman in court now, even though he's a member of our association, he initiated this lawsuit on his own. If he fails in his, then we're going to move forward with our lawsuit. It depends on how the city responds. We're going to get his lawyer with the Institute for Justice doing it *pro bono.*

We are putting out a tour guide handbook. This will be our own publication. We were trying to get city funds for that, but I don't think we're going to get it. I'm on the executive committee of APT and I suggested to our membership that we should not seek outside money for this project. We should get the membership to contribute to the cost of its own publication. That way we don't have to wait for the city or their sanctions on our publication. It's a private publication and tough beans. ▪

Just outside Independence Hall in Philadelphia, Pennsylvania, an actor is reading through his lines to play the part of an 18th century U.S. soldier.

My one-day trip to and from California for my daughter's high school graduation.

Graduation — Saratoga, California

Unfinished housing development — Las Vegas, Nevada

Brooklyn, New York

Thomas

Okay, so I'm walking along Wyckoff Avenue in Brooklyn snapping pictures. I hear someone behind me hailing me, "Hey you!" Damn— now what? A black guy asks if I took his picture. I say no. Then he hits me up for some money. I ask where he's from. He's a Brooklyn native. I give him lunch money, then ask if he'd mind if I did take his picture. He says no, then launches into a tale of how he lives on the streets and how he was shot and how he... Whoa. Hold on. Now it's getting interesting. Thomas rolls up his left sleeve and shows me the entry wound on his left forearm, then asks me to feel the bullet. I feel a lump on the other side of his arm. He says it was a silver bullet, because they thought he was a vampire. I suggest that he have it removed, then sell it for the money. He smiles and begins a series of poses for me to photograph. As I finish up and leave I tell him to watch his back and he tells me to watch mine. ■

Same day. I'm standing underground on a subway platform. This weekend the MTA is working on something-or-other and the schedules are, well, a mess. There's a big white guy near me (and by big I mean I'd-want-him-on-my-side-in-a-fight big). He's complaining vociferously about the subways, the United States, and high taxes. He wants to move to Italy. He's served in the Marines (presumably ours) for twenty-five years. He's been shot three times. (Just what is it with New Yorkers and bullet wounds?) He has just had it with the lack of leadership. (I'm guessing his guy didn't win the last election.) I'm feeling adventurous, so I move closer, but still outside his arm's reach. I mention that I was in Italy the year before and that they have their problems, too. He sizes me up for a moment, then complains more directly towards me about New York. Just then a train arrives. He warmly waves good-bye as he steps aboard. Very New York. No photo. No name. ■

Wall Street — Manhattan, New York

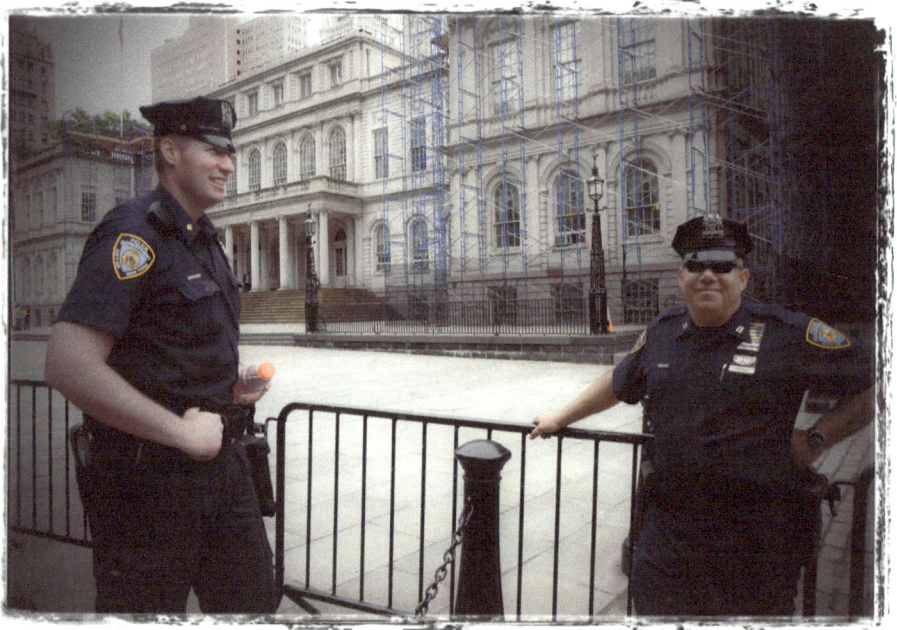

Two of New York's Finest outside City Hall — Manhattan, New York

Giant inflated rat, Wall Street — Manhattan, New York

Wall Street — Manhattan, New York

Gary

Gary had his rig parked at a rest stop off Interstate 80.

I live in Vincennes, Indiana, home of Red Skelton. I drive for a company out of Arkansas and we go anywhere. I'm going to Texas now. I usually don't drive too much beyond Pennsylvania, Delaware, and New Jersey. I've been doing it about six or seven years.

I ask other truckers if it's busy out there. They say they'd rather have a little bit more than what they do. I think everybody's taking it in stride. It hit everybody hard in the beginning. Now it's not so bad. There's a lot of them getting out, though. They're tired of it—all the stuff we have to put up with out here.

Brokers sometimes double-dip, and they take it off the trucker's profit. If you're an owner-operator you make more on the miles, but then you have to think about your maintenance. They say you have to have about $10–15,000 stored up in case you blow an engine or something else. I'm a company driver and that's their rig I'm driving, but I'd like to be an owner. See, if you're an owner operator you have to buy everything, but on your fuel you get a surcharge back. And, actually, when the fuel prices were higher, the owner-operators said the money was better. They got more money back on the fuel. And now diesel's higher in cost. It's like the stock market, you don't know from day to day. ■

Mike and Lori

Mike and Lori had their rig parked at a rest stop off Interstate 80 in Indiana. Lori was adamant about not having her picture taken.

Lori: We've been out of work for the last eight weeks; my husband just had surgery. This is our first trip out, so I really don't know how the freight's moving or anything.

Mike: I've been a driver for seventeen years and we're kind of lucky—we're on a dedicated line from Boston to Los Angeles and back. Freight runs better when it's direct, but with the economy being slow we have two extra stops. Coming back out from Los Angeles is supposed to be direct, but we end up stopping in Columbus to drop off freight.

I'm not an Obama fan. It was an exciting election. I'm actually quite proud of the country for being able to elect a black man into office. I thought that was great. I'm just not a Democrat. I'm not a die-hard Republican. I'll vote for a Democrat on occasion. I'm just not into pulling more blood out of us. We're not even home five days a week; we're out on the road working our tails off. It's just difficult for me.

Lori: It can't be bad forever. ■

Racine, Wisconsin

152

Milwaukee Art Museum — Milwaukee, Wisconsin

Milwaukee, Wisconsin

Glen, Cornell, and Wendell

Glen, Cornell, and Wendell are from Baton Rouge, Louisiana. I met them at the Harley-Davidson Museum in Milwaukee, Wisconsin. They belong to a motorcycle club called the Nubian Kruzers. Recently they did a charity ride to raise money for a battered women's shelter.

Wendell: We're some brothers from Louisiana—riding brothers. We're doing some positive things back there in the community with our motorcycle group.

As far as the economy, we're pretty stable. It's holding its own. A couple of major companies have had some layoffs, but not full-scale layoffs like shutdowns. We have Exxon Chemical's oil refineries there and they haven't had a problem. Dow Chemical had a layoff, which is a huge facility down there, they had like a hundred people laid off just recently. They're still doing good.

Glen: You've got to spend money to make money. The President's philosophy is the stimulus package. People will start spending and it will come back on that basis, although it doesn't seem practical to spend that kind of money. But like I always say, the people making those decisions must know what they're doing. That's how I look at it.

This administration just started. He is trying to recover from President Bush. Me, being a Vietnam veteran. He attacked Iraq because the guy was killing his own people. North Korea's carrying on. We're going to attack North Korea? And also, he said we went in there for weapons of mass destruction. No weapons of mass destruction? Withdraw and get out. Afghanistan is where all our troops ought to be. There's a hidden agenda in Iraq. But me, I like all presidents—all presidents. But when Bush did that move there, I couldn't figure it out. What's the reasoning? Why did you invade this country and not that country? What's the *real* answer?

Wendell: Besides throwing money at the economy, what else is there?

Glen: Are you going to go spend it? Are people going to spend the money? I've heard the Republican Party say cut taxes, cut taxes. Would that make it better? I mean, before you increase spending, cut taxes. I wonder how that would be? Like I say, I'm not a politician. I like all presidents. But why can't we pull out of there right now. To hell with them. That's their country. I'm trying to think of a rational reason. I'm not going to bother you. You run your country. But if you come bother this country, I'm going to tear you apart. I'm not going to dip my nose in Saddam Hussein killing his own people. Do we really care if he kills his own people? I don't think we really care.

Wendell: But the United States has always been like a big brother.

Glen: Yeah. But why?

Wendell: Because that's who we are.

Glen: That's not our relationship.

Wendell: Let's think about it like this—somebody's picking on my brother. What am I going to do?

Glen: Some people would do nothing.

Wendell: I'm going to stand up for you.

Glen: You're going to fight for me?

Wendell: Damn right. Because I know you.

Glen: But if it was Mike Tyson or Shaq doing it to me you'd be hesitant. Right?

Wendell: Me? Well…

Glen: I think rational about attacking certain people.

Wendell: It wouldn't be an attack. It's defending your brother. You're standing up for them when they can't. But Iraqis are building now. Their troops are getting better. So, now it's time to stand away. Now it's time to get out.

Glen: I understand what you're saying. There's an agenda. There's all that oil over there. There's a reason we're not out of there. We're not getting the oil? That's just what they tell you. Look, I was in Vietnam. We finally got out and the communists still took it over. So what did we accomplish by being a big brother? Nothing.

Wendell: Not too much.

Glen: We accomplished nothing. The north still took it over. So what can we hope to accomplish in Iraq? Just get out and use that money elsewhere. Get out of there. Just protect your land. I don't want to mess with nobody. I don't want to be the big brother no more. Nixon got in in '69 and he started taking troops out in '70. But back then there was a protest against us, unlike now—there's nobody in the streets with signs. If they're playing with people's lives—I don't know what they're doing. I don't know what their agenda is.

That's another thing. I try to look at things as fair as I can. Iran's going nuclear—so what? We have it. We're the only country that's ever used it. So, who says they're evil. We say they're evil. Why can't they have nuclear weapons?

Wendell: Israel's the only stable country over there.

Glen: I don't know. I've talked to a lot of Arabic people and they say Israel took their land. And the United States backs them up. I don't think it's fair.

Wendell: The news reporting there—we don't get it here. No. We don't get half of it.

Glen: All we get is a little bit of it.

Wendell: We get the one side, so we can keep supporting Israel.

Glen: I'm sympathetic to any people in bondage. My heart goes out to them—like the Holocaust. That was horrible. But I think the worst crime to mankind was slavery. I think that's the worst crime ever committed. They speak of the Holocaust all the time and six million people; they lost that many coming over here on ships.

(Cornell and Wendell excused themselves and I continued talking with Glen. He began recounting his Vietnam experience.) I have a lot of friends on the wall. I think about it a lot. It brings back memories. It's been forty-two years. It helps me to talk about it. Lately I've been opening up about it. I was just nineteen years old. I saw my eighteen-year old buddy get blown up right next to me. That's the way it goes. I still love America. I love the people in it, not the government—the Constitution; the way it's written up. The people have power in America. Basically, we're still a young nation.

I'm going to go back to Vietnam. It's been on my mind. There's a tour you can take. Five of us said we're going to go. It would be healing. Everything's changed. It's built up. I want to go to the exact place I was at. From there I can visualize how it was. I was there twelve and a half months.

[I asked if he was drafted.] Man, I volunteered! You know why? Because my older brother was a career soldier and I always admired him. I'm going to go over there, but I didn't know. I knew the war was going on, but I was thinking I would be like John Wayne—hide behind a rock and shoot the bad guys. When I got there, it was the biggest mistake. Thank God I survived. I followed my brother. He had twenty-five years and he'd been twice. I told him, sorry, I'm not going back there no more, and I got out. I did my duty.

I could write a book on it for my son. I wouldn't dare tell him, don't go, if America called you in the right way—for someone like Bin Laden. For me, that's worth fighting for. But going to Iraq wasn't necessary.

Cornell didn't really have anything to say. I invited him in on the conversation, but he declined. Once we were outside to take some photos, he looked me up and down and said, "I'll bet you're one of those rich guys." I tried to assure him that I wasn't, that I had just enough money and time to do this project, that I drove an eight-year-old Hyundai, for crying out loud. But he was having none of it. ▪

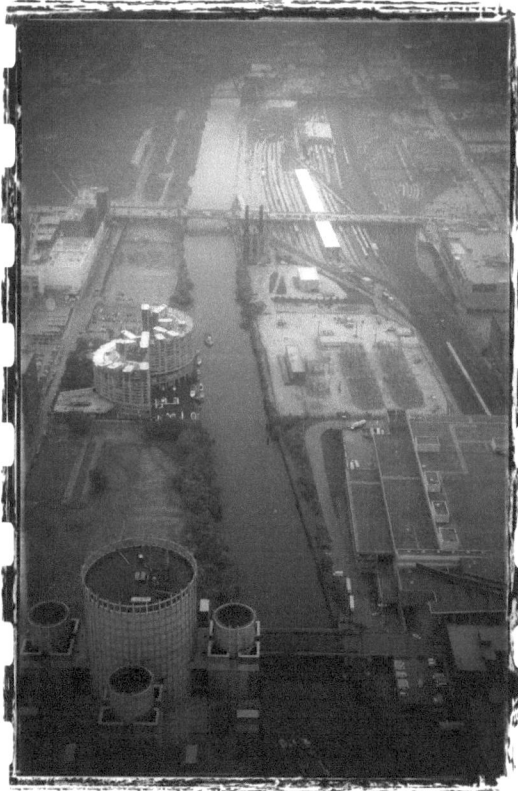

View from Sears Tower — Chicago, Illinois

Strategic Air and Space Museum — Ashland, Nebraska

Abandoned diner — Interstate 80, Nebraska

Roadside distraction — Interstate 80, Nebraska

Giant wagon — Milford, Nebraska

Buford, Wyoming

Don

Buford, Wyoming is the smallest town in the United States. At an elevation of 8,000 feet, it has its own zip code with a population of one. Don owns and runs the Buford Trading Post. He's the one. My car was running on fumes after having just passed through one raucous thunderstorm and he had fuel and conversation. He talked with me in between helping customers. I later looked up Buford on the Internet and saw that it had a population of two at one time. So there's more to the story.

The economy's in the tank—there's no question—because of the politicians. It's that simple. Doesn't matter if it's a Republican or a Democrat. It's the politicians, because they put their agenda ahead of the country and the people. And their agenda is power and money.

I'm a believer in free enterprise. That's why I have my own business. The bottom line is, I want government in my life as little as possible. Many people want government to take care of them. They want entitlements. The only thing I'm entitled to is to breathe. That's the way I feel about it. Keep government out of my life; I'll take care of myself. Let government do the things for me that I cannot do for myself—seal the borders; protect me from getting blown up. Those are the type of things I want government for. I don't want a fascist government, to where I own the business, but they tell me what to do with it, how to run it, what I can price things at. That's why I live here. If I wanted those things, there're plenty of countries that offer that. [Laughs.] I could go live there.

The two-party system works, *if* it's a two-party system. Right now we have a one-party system. They might call themselves Republicans, or they might call themselves Democrats, but the bottom line is, you should have one party over here and another party over here. They have different ideologies on how things should be done and the idea behind that is to meet somewhere in the middle. Now you've got the Democrats here and you've got the Republicans right here—right next to them. They might have a Republican sticker on them, but they're not practicing the Republican ideology of less government, less intrusion in your life.

A third party right now would make it a two-party system. [Laughs.] Just like with Ron Paul—he's another one. To me, he's probably one of the few good congresspeople that we have. I've found that with liberals—and when I say liberals I'm talking more extreme liberals and extreme conservatives, when they're out on the fringes like this— you're hearing more from the extreme liberals now, than you do from the extreme conservatives. And I have a couple of friends that are extreme liberals and I know not to get into any kind of dialog with them, because I have my opinion, they have their opinion, but if my opinion is not the same as their opinion—I'm wrong. It's not that I have a different opinion and they disagree with it—it's that I'm wrong. I think we have arguments because of the fact that we have extreme liberals—you can't have a debate with them, because they already know you're wrong. And why do I want to agree with you if I know you're wrong?

But the right's the same way.

Oh, I don't think so. Maybe the extreme right. I consider myself right. And yes, we used to have dialog. When the parties are separate like that and they want to get something done, they have to find somewhere to compromise, because it's not all you and it's not all me—and we don't have that. Congress has its own agenda; they don't care what the people think. They can't control their spending.

As a civilized society we need government. We need it to keep peace and order, to keep the infrastructure there, but when government is the behemoth that it is now—it's insane. I've got a feeling that when the baby boomers are out of here, this system will collapse. For one, the baby boomers gave birth to the entitlement group. They were so good to them that they didn't teach them what they needed to teach them. So now, the entitlement group has had children and they didn't know what the hell to teach them. I've got one child and he's entitled to everything. He lives on his own and if he doesn't want to starve to death, he has to find a job. This meal wagon is closed.

I sit here and watch all three TV channels of news all day long. I don't just watch CNN, I don't just watch FOX, because as much as I think it's probably the best station in giving me more information, I don't trust that they're giving me all. So I watch CNN to see what stories pop up there compared to that story popping up somewhere else, and try to get a full view. It's like all the focus on the Iranian election— they need to focus on our elections here. There's more fraud probably here than there is there. I don't think our last election was a legitimate election.

I didn't agree with Obama, because what I feared in Obama is coming true. I was hoping I was wrong, but the left agenda that he's pushing...see I don't believe that Obama's a natural-born citizen. Why would he be fighting it? He's spent $800,000 keeping his college transcripts, his birth certificate and other information from the public. You go down and get your driver's license, you've got to produce your damn birth certificate. So why would that be a problem? I called my two congressmen and my one house representative on speed dial. I talk with them several times a month and that was one of the issues I brought up. Why don't they dig into it and find out? I think the reason is that the mainstream media doesn't want to dig into it. This is their boy. And I don't mean boy because he's black—this is their man. They picked their horses in the beginning and he's the one they're running with and they're backing him.

We should not have bailed out anybody. In a free-enterprise system we let them collapse. Why stick twenty billion in it, and then let them go bankrupt? I want what's best for the country and me as a businessperson. If Obama wanted to stimulate the economy all he had to do was to pass a law where I suspend my withholding tax. That would have given my one employee an extra fifty-two dollars a week that she would have spent. Instead, she's got six dollars and fifty-seven cents more with his program. Had you suspended hers that would have suspended my portion of hers, which would give me more money—and it would have given it to me next Friday. And that's not running up the debt; it's not money coming in, but it's not money you're spending. It's zeroing itself out, in a sense. The way he did it, I'm still paying and she's not getting anything and he's still spending a ton of money.

They've all got their fingers in it. I'm not just pointing at Obama. It's politicians in general. If they don't have their fingers in, then they're doing something wrong. The whole system is screwed up. It's the politicians—they're not looking out for the people. That's why I do not vote for incumbents.

I've been here 19 years. Last month I was down thirty-eight percent. That equates to about $32,000. What I'm seeing from people is they come in and buy the necessities, the gas, and they might buy cheap stuff. It started last year. I had this jewelry case full and normally in one summer I could sell out. It's all Native American. It's real silver, real turquoise. I bought this last spring. It's been here for a year and this is what I have left. Normally I'm out by August or September. It runs in spurts.

Up until last year there's been one recorded tornado at 8,000 feet or above. Last year we had three…in the matter of a week. See, I don't believe in global warming, either. I believe in global cycles. There'll probably be another ice age and it doesn't matter if my chimney's puffing out smoke. They should build more nuclear power plants.

[After having given a customer a good-natured hard time.] They might leave cussing, but they'll do it with a smile on their face. I'm open seven days a week. I have a manager that splits the hours with me. I work about twenty-five and she works about forty-two or forty-four— something like that. Eight to six every day.

We have serious problems in this country. And the sad part about it is the only people who can correct it are the people that get elected. I get so many people through here that are just disenchanted, unhappy, they don't like things the way they are. Many of them tell me they don't vote, because their vote does not count. The other ones don't like it, but they keep all of these guys are up there and somebody keeps voting them into office. My father told me years ago, if you don't like the results you're getting on something, you probably ought to change what your doing. So, if we don't like what our congresspeople are doing, why do we keep re-electing them? I've asked people this question and they say they don't know about the new guy. Well, you know the old guy's shafting you, that's a fact. So what's the worst-case scenario, the new guy's going to shaft you too? It's that kind of thinking that just blows my mind. It amazes me. And when you vote, it gives you bitching rights.

My son's like that. He's twenty-five and he says it doesn't do any good to vote. Don't you understand that when you don't vote, you don't cancel out the other guy's vote. You're just giving it to him. And there's so many people in this country that do that. And you can see that by the election turnout. When we have an election and we get thirty-eight percent. Now California just did that. In the presidential election I think California had seventy-seven percent turnout. But then they just had this vote where they wanted to raise taxes—thirty-eight percent. And Schwarzenegger was just on TV; he's cutting the state welfare, because they don't have money for that. And it's basically the kids; it's the kids that aren't going to get the money. You don't hear Schwarzenegger or anyone in political life saying, "Why don't we just cut our salaries?"

Obama was talking with the American Medical Association, and I guess he wants the doctors to take a hit. In my viewpoint, hospitals and medical services have become big business. Hospitals are competing—some look like resorts. I'm not saying that's wrong; that's the free enterprise system. But with a hospital, you go in there—you don't have a choice. You're sick and you have to find someone to help you. That's different than walking into a car showroom and you have Mercedes and Chevy. You know your budget. I grew up in St. Louise and we used to have county hospitals. If you didn't have money you went to the county hospital. They should pay their doctors a competitive wage. People shouldn't die because they're poor. They should have a place to go. I think you should change the whole system to accommodate for that. Instead of being at this extreme, you're over at this extreme. Anytime you're at the extremes, that's where the problems are.

[After having helped a customer.] You just wonder how many people just walk in, then walk out with something. Theft is a big thing. I find it with my sunglasses. I use to keep them in the gift area over there and sometimes I'd find one, two, three of the pricing labels laying on the ground. They'd put the sunglasses on and walk out and you don't know if they walked in wearing them. I moved it over here, so at least when somebody's spinning that thing I can keep an eye on them. You hope you don't lose that much. You can't be naïve to the fact that with all the reports you know retail loses a lot of money to thievery.

The U.S. is stretched so thin. I think we'd be hard-pressed to do much of anything. Because if you have the power and you won't use it—and they know you won't use it, then you don't have any power.

I think that this country should concentrate on solving the problem. Find a way to operate without that damned oil, either by changing automobiles or coming up with a different fuel to where you can tell the Saudis and all those others to start drinking the shit, because it's not good for anything else. And just leave them alone. If they want to go over there and kill themselves, let them kill themselves. When you've got somebody that's just a religious nutcase, there's no reasoning with them. They're working on a different level. All of those Muslims over there believe that any people in the West are the infidels. And because you're in the West, we need to kill you. We went after Iraq and now Iran and we should have gone after Saudi Arabia. But it's all about the oil. Even if they can't find some alternate fuel, we have so many other places in this country that we could drill. ■

Lake Oswego, Oregon

Keith

Keith is a bright entrepreneur and businessman located in Portland, Oregon.

Personally, I'm very pleased with my portfolio going back up with the stock market. It's much better than it was six months ago. For me the economy has been bad since 2000. The whole decade's been a challenge economically in terms of business. I can't say that this time around feels any worse than the 2001 downturn. I was in the tech sector. I had a company with 120 employees and three offices doing software development. One year we were doing twelve million in revenue and the next year, 2000–2001, we were doing four and a half million. I had to lay off two-thirds of my employees and shut down two of the offices. I was barely able to sell the company to pay off creditors. The tech downturn was based on two things: one, there was a bubble in tech, but the more important thing was the free trade policy. All the software development like mine was moved offshore to places like India. So the clients were basically saying we're not going to be working with you any more; we're going to be working with this Indian or Chinese outfit. It would have happened whether it was Clinton or Bush. You can't really blame Bush for that. It was the tech bubble. But the rest of the economy didn't have that bubble.

After that, I tried various ventures. I tried the fashion retail business. Again the same thing. I was trying to import South American, European designs and also U.S. designs, but we got undersold by stuff coming out of China and India in the large chain stores. So, there's this whole trend against small business and local business like me. That's what I experienced in fashion retail. People are extremely sensitive to price. You have pressure on jobs, because a lot of the stuff that used to be produced here moved overseas, but on the other hand it's been good for the consumer—now they pay a lot less.

You drive a Hyundai and since you made that choice you end up with General Motors and other companies going bankrupt. People can blame General Motors, and to a degree I would—it was a mismanaged company. The fact is that when we were growing up there were a lot more middle-class jobs. We drove lousy cars. Everybody remembers the old Chevys and Fords as being good cars, but they were really lousy cars from the fifties and sixties. It was a planned economy and the money circulated through society. Anyway, this whole focus on the consumer means we got dirt-cheap TVs, stereos, calculators, and even automobiles. Now there's a lot less idle-class jobs; there's the wealthy on top in finance and service workers at the bottom. I'm in business. I've been in business for twenty years—a small businessman—and it's been a struggle. I did management consulting for the past couple of years and I did okay with that, but I've seen that quiet down, too. Actually, I know a lot of management consultants that were maybe more successful than I was and the past six months is the first time they've really been out of work. There's less demand. First, you have the energy crisis, so people started spending less money on retail and other services and diverting more money to energy, and that caused an economic downturn for people earning money in those sectors, and that caused the housing bubble to go down, and that caused the whole banking crisis that we know about. It's an economic challenge.

The broader theme for me is the complete, unfettered open markets. Other countries do it for their own economic benefit and the U.S. lets it go for free. Other don't really do that. When you look at the software engineers that might be earning a quarter of the U.S. salary, it's just really an exchange rate. When they're in their own local countries they live in very nice houses, maybe even have servants. Someone who makes $15,000 there has a much better lifestyle than someone who earns

$60,000 in the U.S. So what does that mean? It's an exchange rate. If you moved the exchange rate up so that the same amount of labor was the same in each country, there wouldn't be this big movement overseas.

Everybody says it's going to be the century of China. I have some confidence in the leadership in Washington under Obama. There is concern about forward price/earning ratios in the stock market—that there's going to be another stock market tanking that's going to be really bad for retirement. One of the problems in our society is that we do consume too much. People buy too much junk that they don't need. People are stopping doing that, which is the economy, to some degree. Another thing is that we're going to have a cyclical energy situation, because energy supplies are running out—peak oil and all that. The moment oil goes up it depresses the economy, then the price goes back down. I think it's going to be tough for our economy to recover, because of the energy situation, and I don't think American society is going to become savers rather than consumers. The world needs some profligate society like we used to be to drive consumerism so they can sell all the goods. That's been the strategy of China, Korea, and all these countries. We'll sell all this stuff to Americans. They'll let us consume, but they save there. And they've been able to drive economic growth. I think it's ingrained in them to save. I think one of the reasons we've had a lot of economic growth is that we do spend our money. And there's a certain optimism around that. ■

Brian

In his mid-twenties, Brian had recently moved out of the banking sector.
No photo.

We would handle unemployment for the state of Oregon at our bank. They wouldn't send you a check, you'd get a debit-like card—a ReliaCard Visa—that they'd load the money onto. We went from two or three ReliaCards a day in early 2007 up to forty a day recently. It's skyrocketed.

It's plastic. You pull your money out of an ATM, it's two bucks. If you check your balance more than twice a month, it costs five dollars. Our bank has the biggest ATM network in the state. According to policy, if somebody comes into the bank and wants a copy of their statement, it would cost them seven bucks. You can only go on our bank's website for free for ninety days. I've run so many statements for free for people, so I could go right around that. They would just nickel and dime you on everything.

Our computer system's smart enough to decline that debit card— sorry, not enough money. But no, we'll pay so you're not embarrassed at the checkout stand, then we'll hit you for an extra $35 per item. You can tell the bank not to give you overdraft protection, but you have to go in and set it up. Half the time they'll fight you on it. They'll say it can't be done. You tell them you don't want any overdraft limit on your card; that you want you're overdraft limit set to zero.

I've had people come in saying that they bought six items and each item has an overdraft charge, like $250 of overdraft fees. They can't pay that. It's an opt-out system now. It's national.

There's another thing that banks will do in how they process your charges. Most banks now will process them from the biggest to the smallest, assuming you want your mortgage payment to be paid as opposed to your McDonald's purchase. So, when all your items come in to the bank for the day you take the biggest one first. That one wipes out your account, so that the smaller ones generate more overdraft fees. That's going to change, so that banks will have to process them as they get them. That was the main one that I'd see on a daily basis. People would come in with three hundred dollars of overdraft fees and I'd be embarrassed. But it's even worse. If in four days you haven't paid the overdraft fees, they add on seven bucks a day until you pay it off. It will continue to accrue at seven dollars a day for forty-five days, then it will charge off and you have about nine months to pay it off, then it goes to a collection agency. I once saw eight dollars in charges generate a thousand dollars in fees. That's when people are buried. Then they try and get an attorney to fight it. ■

Portland, Oregon

Chandra

I stumbled across Chandra banging away on a set of drums in a small garage in Portland, Oregon. She sings in bands on and off. The drums are her roommates.

I got booted out of my lease where I had a salon chair, because they raised the rent to make up for the economy. So I started working out of my basement, which cut my clientele in half. It keeps me home a lot and my neighbor says I don't have a job, because I work from home. She sees me all the time. She's nosy. She's probably in her late thirties—early forties. She's covered in tattoos just like me and has black hair, so I know she's been where I am.

I just recently got a job at a high-end salon, hoping to pick up a new clientele and actually make a living. And in the meantime, I'm just trying to assert myself as a grown-up and have my own home and not have so much drama. I don't think she knew how old I was. She thought she could come over here and bully me for a little while about my cat's behavior and me playing drums in the garage, but I think she was surprised.

When times are lean, people fall back on their music. And it's really frustrating when somebody comes by and tells you that you can only make a certain amount of noise or the noise she appreciates. She's told us that the noise she's heard so far is that we are a shitty band. She hasn't actually heard me, she's only heard my roommate, but I thought that was kind of a low blow. She came over and said, "Well you guys suck, anyway."

You know, everybody has the right to make music. It's artistic. You can be creative. Who can afford to have extra practice space? There's a reason it's called a garage band. It's just frustrating. We're not breaking any rules. She lives in the renovated portion of this apartment complex. It's owned by the same people. The people over there think that all the people over here are terrible pet owners and things like that. They're still just rentals. Everybody that lives here is a bartender except for me.

I'm sure she knows I drink every once in a while. I mean, where are we supposed to live? What are we supposed to do? We don't fit into her little mold of what should be happening. I want everybody to get along. We don't really do anything too crazy. We don't make noise after certain hours.

I'd like to own a home in Portland. I really like it here. I'm a stylist, so I'll probably keep it up. Hopefully, I'll have a clientele that will keep me going with this salon. I also have some leads on doing hair while bands are in town. My friend does make-up and lights for all the shows that come in. I'm really hell-on-wheels as far as, like, hair. I'm going to the Warp Tour. We'll see what happens. One way or another this thing is viable, even if I have to share it with other people to pay the mortgage. It's a really good time to buy. ■

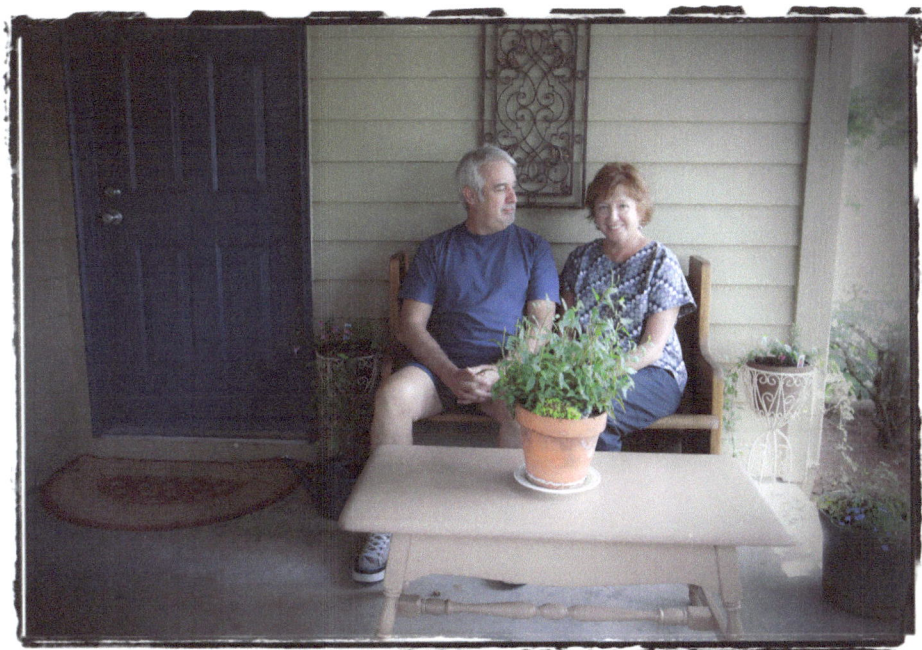

Lake Oswego, Oregon

Mark and Angie

Mark and I grew up across the street from each other in Southern California. We played in a rock band together in high school and have remained friends to this day. At the time of this interview, Mark was unemployed. Angie is a nurse at a VA hospital.

Mark: I think we're going to come back. Eighteen months to two years. I don't like the house-of-cards thing that happened. Something went wrong, then something else went wrong, and then everything just folded after that. I don't understand that at all. I don't like that part of the economy. I do understand it, in the sense that we made a lot of bad loans. We live in a false economy. We have a real bad ego problem about being rich, about having money. As an insurance agent many years ago in Carlsbad, California, thinking these people have this false image about how much money they have. This was twenty years ago. Back then the real estate went down, but the economy was fine. [To Angie] You work for the government. You must have something to say about it.

Angie: The only thing that government employees are affected by is their Thrift Savings Plan—their TSP. That's their retirement fund. The stock market has gone in the toilet and now people are saying they have to work five years longer, because they've lost money—when they didn't lose money, they just didn't make it. It's not a loss until they cash out, but they think they lost out. They need to move it and they need to move it into secured money.

Mark: Even when the economy was cooking, I was not happy with a lot of it. I still thought it was a false economy. And I'm not an economist. I'm not that educated in business. I don't even like business. I love America, but I really don't like this. I thought people were cocky and arrogant.

Angie: Here's my sad economic story. I had $30,000 invested in a home from the sale of a house and I bought a larger house with that with a business partner. We were going to keep it five years and put it back on the market. So, we had the house on the market for one year and we had no offers. This was just this last January. Then it went off the market.

It did not sell, so I opted to get out of the financial agreement and give back my investment to my partner. I am no longer invested in the house, because the house is not going to sell. I gave away my $30,000. I chose to do that. Nobody's buying. Three years ago the house was appraised at $335,000 and today it's appraised at $275,000. It was originally bought for $263,000.

San Francisco, California

Mayra

Mayra's café is not far from Union Square in San Francisco. She's been running it for the past five years. This year, several of her regular customers have stopped by to say good-bye—that they had been let go from their jobs and would not be coming back. Mayra believes her business is down thirty percent (a similar figure to that cited by others in their interviews). She was hoping for an increase in business during the summer tourist season. ■

.

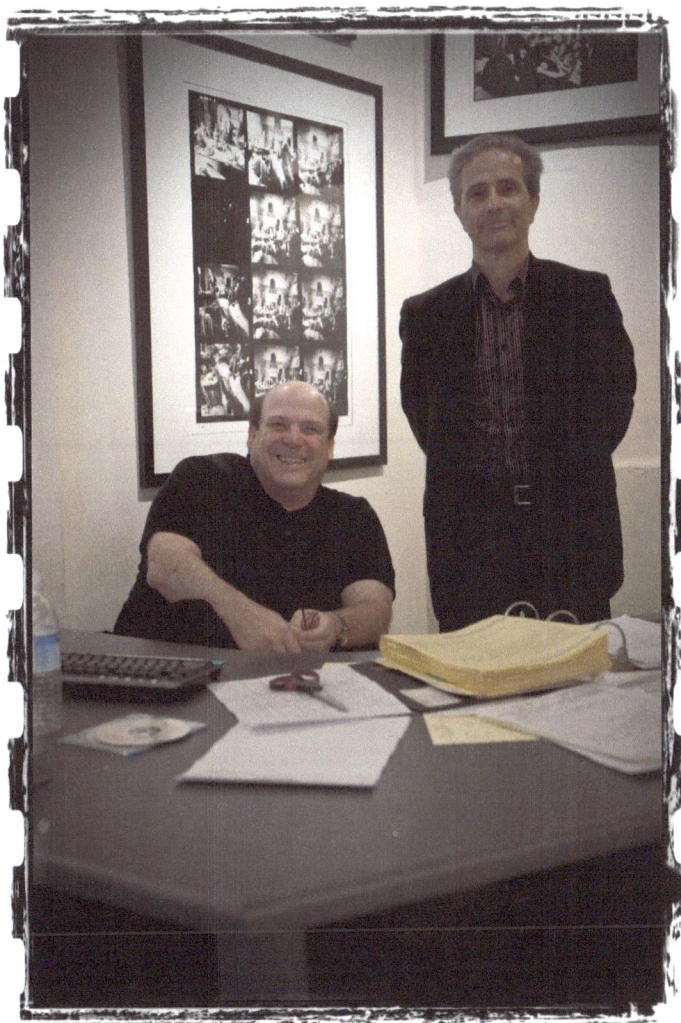

San Francisco, California

Jim and Theron

I worked with Jim and Theron at an art gallery nearly thirty years ago. They have owned their own gallery, the San Francisco Art Exchange, for the past twenty-five years. I interviewed them separately.

Jim

I see the economy from a business point of view. Beyond that it's just listening to people babble on TV. No matter which side you're on, they both seem to be wrong. I can only relate to it in terms of my own business, because that's not Disneyland. I'm the one selling. I'm responsible for selling. I'm seeing it person by person.

Simply put, the lower end of the business is terrible and the upper end of the business has been good. Our thirty-to-forty-thousand-and-up business has saved us. At the lower end of the totem pole, our two-, three-, and four-thousand-dollar, which has historically been our bread and butter, has been greatly damaged by this economy. How much of that is confidence versus capability? Generally, I get the feeling that most people interested in buying at the lower level are fearful. They're keeping what they have just in case. A lot of people are in businesses, their cash flow is based on business bucks that they did six months ago; money's still flowing in, but the new business is bad.

Why the upper-end business is better? One can only guess. What I've seen is that people who have wealth, have assets of cash—they have money. They still took a hit. And some of those people were of a mind that they just watched thirty percent of what they had evaporate and what we deal with here pretty much appeals to that cultural level. Some of these people are saying, "I could have spent that thirty percent on this piece of art. Now I have something I really enjoy. And it has historic value, too." The other side of the coin, and probably more appropriate to the situation is that people who have some dough, this is the time to have clout. And we've been particularly good at working with our sources to get people to be flexible with their prices, so we're able to offer good deals to people. At the upper end is where it's really effective.

We sell almost nothing on-line—but we get a lot of leads from our Internet site. We get some passive business—an inquiry, an email. But we do a substantial amount of business that we can track back to the Internet. Directly, orders over our website are less than one percent. It really is minor. Think about it. You're looking at a website and someone's thinking about spending $3,000—and some people do that—usually they want to see if you're living and breathing on the other end.

Last September is when the lower-end business dropped off. I very purposely changed my focus to go after the big ones. I realized very quickly that that was where it was going to be, if we were going to somehow make it through this thing. So we were very aggressive about going out and finding more valuable things to sell at reasonable prices. We worked with our sources and our clients. We didn't hide the fact that things were sticky. In fact, we used that as a plus for buyers to buy—you can really grab some treasures at a great price. We've taken a value-for-the-dollar approach and concentrated on it. And that strategy has worked so far.

Some people think the worst hasn't even started yet. I don't know. I'm not smart enough—or dumb enough. I don't know which it is. I do think the public's been living in a fantasy relative to their well-being. Going back three or four years, I recall that my daughter had a best friend whose younger brother was in the second mortgage business leveraging home equity. This kid didn't know much; he was just really gutsy. He'd call anybody up. He was making James Bond money. He had a great car, a great house, the best furniture—just making truckloads of money. When I saw this kid with no experience making that kind of money, living that kind of lifestyle, I just thought there's something really wrong here.

There're people that say the government started this idea, that we want everybody to have a home. They lowered the standards and they put pressure upon the lending institutions to sell more houses. I think that's totally true. I don't think that's all that's true. It's just one of the things. There's the victim's side of it—you made me buy this house. But I come from the school that in this life you'd better figure out how to be responsible for yourself. I don't have a lot of pity.

There could be a healthy adjustment from all this. We're so materialistic—we can do anything we want and pay for it when we want to. We always think things are going to get better. And I like that about America, that we have that positive outlook. But at some point that positive view turned into something more, like people making thirty grand a year can buy that $600,000 house. At some point it just goes beyond. There's got to be something structural causing that, at various levels. It's never having a full dose of reality.

I'm an optimist. I can't help it. My optimism runs to the fact that I feel I can do what I need to do to maintain. I'm not attempting to take the world on my shoulders. I have a feeling that we're uniquely positioned in what we're doing and we'll continue to ride out the storm—and it's a perfect storm. We've been hit that way before. We have something different and we've been in business a long time. We're the top gallery in the world for what we do. So we have access to more things than galleries of the same bent have access to—in the six figures repeatedly. Many other galleries don't have the relationships and access that we do. To go out and make a $125,000 sale to save the month, other folks don't even have that or have a clue as to how and go get it. We know where the stuff is, because we've sold it for the past several decades. Lately, we've been buying it back from people that are a little low now and they're willing to sell it for reasonable prices. We sell it to new people who can afford it. Still it's a deal for them. But there are practical limits for how long you can draw on that. You're drawing it down a little bit as you go. We're reaching out, too. We're spending a lot of money on advertising. Part of that is being financed with some of these deals we're making. Hopefully that will work out.

Theron

I'm an art dealer and this is my thirtieth year in San Francisco. My business partner and I started the gallery in 1983. Being an art dealer is not your average business. It's unpredictable. You're selling things that people don't see as utilitarian. You're almost always presenting things based on intangible benefits. I've been through a number of recessions, a lot of cycles, every one is different—this one, for some reason, I'm not so troubled by. I'm challenged.

After 9/11 was pretty devastating. Business came to a standstill. You could play Frisbee in the middle of Geary Street because there were no cars. Our overhead was eating us alive. We were digging a deep hole trying to stay in business. Once things started to improve I vowed that I was not going to be held hostage to various things in business. I wasn't going to be held hostage to a temp updating our website when it needed to be updated. I wanted to have control of that at any time, because the whole idea, in any business I suppose, is communication—to have as much versatility in communication as possible, because the more people you talk to, the more people will do business with you.

Think of every icon you can think of, whether it's images of Marilyn Monroe or photographs of James Dean. There are things here that are continuing to find their way here, either because I'm digging them up or they're coming to us. We handle about fifty photographers, painters, and illustrators who all created popular icons.

Our record year was 2005. It was the biggest year we ever had in our business by far. It came back from 2001, 2002 when we would have been lucky to break $950,000 for the year. That's sales, not profit. We don't have any money in the cookie jar at that number. In 2003 we did an album cover show that sort of helped raise us up. In 2005 we broke $3,000,000. And some of those sales were a result of people finding us on-line. People were buying from us without ever having been to San Francisco, let alone been to our gallery. It was virtual traffic. More staff had the ability to communicate with various clients by e-mail. 2006 was a little below 2005. We brushed up against $3,000,000. In 2007 we started a soft decline. At the end of that year I was starting to worry. Sales in certain months were pretty tepid. In 2008 we were battling up and down. The first part of the year was looking bleak. The dollar was weak, foreign currencies were strong, so most of our entire quarter was sales outside the country. We hardly did any business with Americans in the first quarter of 2008. It was all in Pounds, Euros. It was a buyers market in foreign currencies, so we had a great first quarter last year and it carried over into the second quarter. The American market was still shaky for lots of reasons, as we well know. We've been through the past eight years and there's lots of reasons for it being shaky. 2008 was an election year, so there was a lot of oxygen sucked out of the air based on things going on in that election. I was politically active all those eight years, exchanging e-mails, communicating with members of the White House, senators and representatives, telling them what I thought. By 2007 I ramped it up and was much more active and more aggressive by pointing out numerous deficiencies, so numerous that they can't be cataloged in this conversation. In 2008 I began working on the Barack Obama campaign. I did a lot of private kind of stuff, as well as working over at the Obama office. I did a lot more blogging. If Macain and Palin had gotten in…there are so many reasons that that should never have happened, but it was very close. I think that's why a lot of us worked so hard to make sure the election results were so that if even some of the votes fell off the table there would be too many to deny. The reason I say that is after the election I felt a lot more hopeful. I knew that things were not going to be perfect. I knew that when your ship is going in the wrong direction (falling into a metaphor here), I knew that to move a big ship you might flip it if you turn too far too fast—you'd sink it basically. So, you're taking on water and going the wrong direction—a new president must be able to move it a few degrees, and it's going to take a long, wide curve to change direction, and there will be some mistakes along the way.

I'm hopeful about Obama. I discuss, I argue, I pursue, I debate with all parts of the political spectrum—far right, far left, communists, socialists, nut-bags, people of good will that really care about stuff. Going into the game-playing metaphor is the way I visualize it. There are parallels symbolically as to what's going on. If you're playing the games on a checker board, it's flat. You have these red and black pieces on it and you're moving forward. There's not a lot of diversity. You're just moving forward. And, for a long time, a good checkers player for the first half of the last century was pretty decent. It was regimented. Communication wasn't as it is today. I can always look at the Bush administration as the era that our leaders still thought we were playing checkers. They came to a chess match asking themselves what the heck are those weird pieces on the board? How hard can it be? We'll move them around the board like checkers pieces. And the game got screwed up. That's how I watched what they were doing. I'm no expert. I'm just trying to understand why things got so weird. Why are we invading a country against the charter of the U.N. that we crafted. It doesn't make sense. We wrote the rule book and now we're breaking our own rules. And not to be conspiracy-like, but I believe that they knew there was no evidence. How is it that there's suddenly a blackout on information? How could we not know that they didn't have weapons of mass destruction? Well, he's just a bad guy. They kept inventing reasons. And every time they invented a reason, it was another hundred billion dollars going someplace that nobody really knew. And nobody was really complaining. The people complaining now were the ones that were writing checks the whole time. Sure, send another hundred billion, two hundred billion, we have to fight for freedom. And all that other branding and re branding of purposes is all part of that hypocrisy and corruption that we live with.

Gray Davis was recalled for a lot less than we have going on in California now. And I wasn't a Gray Davis fan—in fact I'm not really leaning heavily on Schwarzenegger. I'm looking at the overall problem that we have: Enron sucks a bunch of energy money out of California; Cheney says he's going to run the country just like a company. Well, you look at Enron, then you look at the United States. There's a connection. Of course, it was run like a company, just like an Enron or a WorldCom—into the ground. A bankrupt company is what they ultimately did. I've deviated somewhat, but it's all interconnected. We haven't been playing chess for a long time. Checkers is obsolete. Flat chess is obsolete. We're moving into an era of 3-D chess. Everybody's looking at the bottom floor, saying, "You can't move the bishop over here, because your opponent's going to take your knight. Wait a second, take a look at the third floor up and watch the piece I'm moving up there. I have to do this, so this other thing can go over here and capture their king." I hate the fact that this is all war metaphor, because that's what chess and checkers are, but if you look at strategy, there're a lot of people on the left and right judging Obama from the bottom floor. There are things taking place that are not visible to the naked eye. The idea of judging the player based on one level is missing the possibility that there may be other things going on that we're not aware of. My wife and other people are sort of nailing Obama all the time. He may be making advances we don't even see.

Politically my business partner, Jim, and I are on opposite ends. The interesting thing about that is that we don't talk a lot of politics, but sometimes we talk about social things. When I discuss issues that matter to me, I try to discuss them on the basis of mutual benefit. Part of the way we've been able to operate is that we try to focus on the big goals relative to keeping our business open, because if our business isn't running, all that other stuff doesn't matter. So we focus on things that we have individual strengths in. We made that decision at another recessionary period. We used to run the company equally on the same basis—both on the sales floor, both in the office. This was the early '90s, but about mid-to-late '90s we were in a deep hole. It was another recessionary period and it was tough, so we decided to divide and conquer. We started the company over, in the figurative sense. So in 1995 we divided up the duties, so Jim took over the sales staff, direct sales—everything sales related. He has a greater strength at that than I do. I took over finance and marketing—relationship and business development. 1995 was our beginning of the exploration of the Internet. We went online for the first time in 1996. The operational model was a hodgepodge before that. It was all over the map. About 1997 I built relationships that focused on rock photography. It seemed like it was a cool, fun thing and it gained mass. Our fame and public image is now based on this niche. And we're now seen as worldwide pioneers for this.

You can't move a piece without affecting every other piece. Things aren't happening fast enough in Obama's first one hundred days or two hundred days. I think he's moving every piece based on the consequences. You don't move anything without recognizing what the ramifications are. A lot of people are saying why don't we do this now. Strategically, you can't ask for a better time to drive through a single-payer health care plan. That is one of those pieces that radiates out into the economy. Companies are shut during strikes based on health care alone. Handle that and you could make the companies more comfortable.

There are intended consequences and unintended consequences, like replacing the elected leader of Iran in 1953 with the Shah. We're paying for it now, and we're paying for it again and again, and the people in Iran are paying for it, based on meddling, when we don't need to be meddling. In this three-dimensional chess world, that's ancient history. The age of empire is going away and we're moving into a new age where no one's going to be controlling everybody, because we're all holding hands anyway. That's idealistic sounding, but the reality is that it's territories, borders, and resources—they're all those things that people fight over. Back in the days of survival, you'd go after various resources so your tribe would survive. We still live in the age of advanced tribes. The evolution of the species will eventually move to the idea that tribalism is old hat—now there's something called *coopertition*. It's existed in the corporate world for at least ten, fifteen years. I've got competitors in this business, but we cooperate, too. The idea of a to-the-death kind of competition is a waste of time. It doesn't do anybody any good.

All that stuff is still survival instinct based on tribal relationships. That's what gangs are—the Norteños and Sureños are, the Bloods and the Crips, Republicans and Democrats. They want to find meaning, and the problem is they're looking for love in all the wrong places. ■

Scotts Valley, California

Bill

Bill might have been the lone Republican in a sea of Democrats and Independents.

I've been unemployed for about three months. For twelve years I did personal computers—supply chain, manufacturing. Right now I'm looking for a job. They trimmed their business just like others. Everybody's in a similar situation.

I was a manager, so I had to lay off people and close facilities, and then there wasn't space for me, unfortunately. About a year ago I saw it coming. It wasn't a surprise. I started job hunting at the beginning of the year. I needed to stay there, though, and kind of wind down my team. I wanted to make sure that it ended well for everybody. I thought that was my responsibility to my people…

That's a good quality.

…and they paid me a little bit more money to stay.

That's a good quality, too.

The job prospects are slim. I'm at the director level, which is just below VP. I do a lot of work. I generally manage managers, so I have seventy to eighty people working for me. To find a similar type of job takes some time. The economy's not there. It's slow. The opportunities aren't there.

I keep hoping that things are going to get better. I see more light. By nature I'm an optimist, but I'm just not seeing positive things for it to turn around. Obviously I want it to, but I'm just not seeing it. Maybe I'm in the wrong position. It's slow for a lot of people.

I'm a little disillusioned by where our political leadership has taken us over the years. I'm a Republican. I think one of the most frustrated group of individuals you'll find are unemployed Republicans. (laughs) We're not just a little bitter, you know. I don't see these guys taking us in the right direction. Honestly, in a lot of ways I'm glad President Obama was elected. The racial thing, I think it's just marvelous. It's a major milestone for our country. I feel great for the country for that. I think that puts a lot of the bitter racial issues behind us—not all of them, but it's a huge step. I have high hopes. I'm a more fiscally conservative person and more socially moderate. I would do other things for the economy.

I believe in people. And I believe people in small business, big business, working people are going to get us out of this mess. It's not going to be government. Government doesn't create value; it shouldn't be the nanny-state. Some people see government as the solution, as the creator of value. But it isn't.

I'm one of those evil guys who moves jobs around. I'm a supply-chain guy. I put work where it can most effectively be done. I was in the PC business. I moved stuff to China or Mexico. It's where you can be most competitive. It's about winning. A lot of people make it into a morality play—and it's not. It's about surviving economically. You've got to move the production cost. That's how business survives. We're making this country a lot less competitive, a lot less appealing for jobs. That's what I have a problem with. We need to go the other direction and make this country a great place to do business. That's how you create jobs—not with Keynesian economics, by throwing money at it to create jobs. I'm frustrated. I don't see us taking the right steps. Clearly the economy, well I don't see it turning around despite the fiscal stimulus. That's where I'm at on the economy.

I'll be okay. I'm being selective about what I'm looking for—at least at this point. I have a lot of accomplishments on my resume. In a normal economy I would be snapped up very quickly. I don't want to take a step backwards. I'm kind of at the bottom of the executive ladder and that ladder means a lot of money. I'll be frank with that. And staying on that ladder means a lot of money. So I don't want to get off. It's money.

Again, the Republican Party—it's just crazy. I'm socially moderate. I can deal with the variety of lifestyles. Just do what you want to do. I don't care. Fine. But the socially conservative elements of the Republican Party—it's just devastating. It's made it such an unappealing place for people who want to be fiscally responsible, who want small government, but the Republican Party is just so awful because of the social conservatives. I have a tough time stomaching it. My mother gave up. She used to be a Republican woman. She was a Barry Goldwater kind of gal. That's what I love. That's the kind of Republican I am— not this crazy, moral-majority, right-wing nut job. The path they're on is alienating the vote. It's a losing proposition. If they're going to be competitive, they have to reposition themselves. Otherwise, they're going to be the minority party forever.

I would prefer that the Republican Party do it on their own, rather than relying on Obama to fall on his face. But I think he's going to fall on his face tragically, and I think it's really too bad, because I would like the first African-American president to be a success. I think he's more akin to FDR, and I don't think FDR was a successful president. We had a mammoth recession/depression for eight years and he didn't get us out of it.

What we need is for business to see this as a great place to invest and government needs to get out of the way. I think there's a vast majority in this country that is fiscally conservative, that thinks that smaller government is better government, but they're socially more moderate— that's the winning proposition. A lot of it comes down to our primary system. I think it's one of the most destructive things. That divides

Democrats to the left and Republicans to the right. The one tie that wasn't the case was the recall election here in California for governor. It was five candidates who were more moderate.

Before I came here, I worked on the space program. And group-think was always something we avoided after the Challenger incident. I think that global warming is the biggest piece of group-think in the history of man. The science isn't there. The evidence that there's global warming is iffy and then linking it to what man's doing is even more iffy. You've got to resolve all the temperature measurement things. Yes, the ice floes are getting smaller in some areas, but they're getting bigger in others. I think there's enough doubt if it's happening and when you see doubt bringing it up, you see it being stamped out. I'm an engineer and I have a living fear of big science and politicians. Big science is the funding engine, so it's about fear—you get funding by perpetuating fear. The more fear; the more funding. You get the Al Gore effect. The whole thing is just unhealthy and it doesn't seem real to me. I find it revolting. So, there you go. I'm very much in the minority on this point.

When you're going to change your economy to combat global warming, well I have a real problem with that. It should be based on science that's empirical, rather than theoretical or model space, which is a bunch of crap. I used to play with models; you can make them say whatever you want. I fear for science; I really fear for science. It's not good for science to be politicized in this way. Science to me is sacred. It seeks the truth—and we are not seeking the truth at all. The truth and opposing viewpoints are stamped out. And that's bad.

Leadership is poor. None of them have our interests at heart. After 9/11 the good feelings lasted about a year, then it became very partisan again. I think Bush blew it in a lot of ways, but it was a two-way effort,

I think. It's corrupt; it really is corrupt—or corrupting. I don't know. It's very frustrating.

In my time off, I've been reading a lot of history. The founding of this country was very divisive. There were competing ideologies. And that's healthy, I think. You have to have some civilized forum. I think the difference now is that we don't know how to handle it—it's the media. The media has changed so much. The speed at which information is disseminated is, well, JFK's indiscretions would be front page now. I don't know what's healthy. Is it healthy to know about it? It's these morality plays. I get sick of it. I get sick of it on the right; I get sick of it on the left. Please, give me a break. There're so many examples—the hypocrisy involved. Maybe good leaders get filtered out in the process.

And our real focus should be not on the Middle East, but China. It will be interesting to see how it comes out. And we'll all have a front-row seat.

Fourth of July — Hawaiian Theme — Scotts Valley, California

Jennifer and Lisa

I interviewed and photographed this charming lesbian couple. They've been together for eight years and are legally married. The day after the interview I received an e-mail from them regarding their participation. I complied with their wishes.

Hi J,

Lisa and I appreciate our conversation that we had with you and appreciate what you are doing to bring economic awareness to our country, etc. However, on further reflection, we ask you to only use our first names, ▮▮▮▮▮▮▮▮▮▮▮▮▮▮▮▮▮▮▮▮ ▮▮▮▮▮▮▮ *and not to use our picture in your book. You can use our conversation to bring awareness and insight to others, but even living in a liberal area surrounded by wonderful people, we do not want to compromise our family in any way what so ever.*

Our family's safety and well-being comes first, and, unfortunately, we do not want our family exposed in any way that may compromise them. I am sure you can understand our position. We thank you and would like to respectfully ask you to please mail us back the waiver we signed.

Thank you again,

Jennifer

Jennifer: I'm a teacher.

Lisa: And I'm a school principal. We're at different schools.

Jennifer: We met at a similar project that we worked on for the county. Yes. We're legally married—one of 18,000.

Lisa: We were one of the lucky ones. [Pause.] You asked about the economy. As a school principal, every time I turn around there's another several-million dollar cut to education. It means doing with less. The parents have been very generous, so we don't lose music and things like that.

Jennifer: We're working our way through as a family. I'm going to work a little bit extra, but it's hard. We've had to cut back. My salary's not been cut, because I have tenure, but teachers never get a cost of living raise; we're still behind.

How do you see the school system five years from now?

Jennifer: I hope we have PE again and more music and art, aides in the classroom, a lot of extracurricular activities, so the school is like it used to be. I know a Special Ed teacher who spends about $800 a year of her own money on her class.

You have to have hope and just keep moving forward. You cut back on the things you can and just try your best. If you don't have hope, it's kind of bleak. I don't know. The President has so much to handle. So we just try to take care of ourselves and our family.

Lisa: We try to give back to the community.

We talked about Proposition 8 in California. It passed, and decreed a ban on gay marriage, and was upheld by the state's Supreme Court.

Jennifer: I think a lot of it has to do with the size of the state. I really do. They're trying to push it up to the Federal level, like in *don't ask, don't tell.* There's this really amazing, decorated officer who fought in Iraq—knew Arabic—he said, "What I learned was that I need to be honest." So he was honest and he got kicked out. The military discharged him and the words they used were horrible, like he was some decrepit person. He's trying to fight it at the federal level.

It doesn't make sense. We just do what we can within our community and push ourselves a little bit more, even though it makes us uncomfortable, so that we can do our part. It's pretty easy to do that here, but we always think about people in other states. It can be very dangerous for them to just talk about their family.

Lisa: I always think of it in education. I work with middle school kids, and they're evolving into their own adulthood, and they're questioning all kinds of things. I look at them as they look at Obama. They can now aspire to something completely different. I don't need to wave the rainbow flag and all that. I figure there are people at my school that know their principal's gay and I hope that they respect me. Somewhere along the way they will challenge that and think that I like her; that she meant something. She was a good leader. And they do that. I watch them do that. I've never had a kid say a derogatory thing to me in twenty years. I just live my life. I love kids. I respect kids. That's a more important message than driving in with a rainbow flag every day. They can't relate to that. They close down their ideas about it.

Jennifer: We appreciate people who do that, but it's not our style.

Lisa: Showing up with my family at school speaks louder than any kind of political message that a fifteen-year-old could hear at that time in their life. I've found that to be very successful in shifting attitudes and beliefs—with the parents, too.

Jennifer: We're close to fifty, and it's a very stifling lifestyle, unfortunately. It's hard being gay in this country.

Have you come out to your parents?

Lisa: I was raised Catholic.

Jennifer: I was raised Catholic, too. I never, ever thought my dad would talk to me again. Now he sees me as a human being, and they totally embrace our family. So does my mom—she always did. It was a little harder for him. He's a real Christian, Catholic. He struggles, but he chose his daughter over dogma. It's not easy. It probably wasn't easy for Christ either. But we are embraced. It's important to us. We're very lucky.

Lisa: I remember we went on a trip for our honeymoon—not when we got married recently, but when we had a commitment ceremony years ago, before you could get married.

Jennifer: To let our families know we were serious.

Lisa: We went on this trip that was a women's sponsored retreat. And we talked with these couples from Tennessee and Arkansas—all across the country, where they just...

Jennifer: They had to pretend every second.

Lisa: They were so closeted.

Jennifer: We kept growing and moving forward. We can't have any shame. We want to be stronger and stronger. We have to be. People treat us the same. People aren't looking at us twice.

Lisa: They may be.

Jennifer: But you don't see it as much.

Lisa: But it's scary, though. Both of us are very respected people in our professions. But I know, in the back of my mind, and have known for my entire career, if a person were ever looking for a place to hang their hat—it wouldn't matter how effective I was, that's where they would hang their hat. I remember when I was first hired. I had only been on the job a week, when somebody called the school and said, "Do you know you've hired a lesbian?" Luckily, my superintendent was somebody who was very smart and together and said, "I'm fairly certain I knew that when I hired her, so what's your point?" See what I'm saying? If you make somebody mad…well, unfortunately you live with that extra stress. It's like picking at a little scab. Even though it has nothing to do with how effective you are or how hard you work…

Jennifer: It's scary out there, not just for that, but for other things. Our names aren't hyphenated, but I'm thinking about it. Just so there would be no question. Say there was an emergency. We're now carrying our marriage certificate in our wallets along with our driver's license, because we don't have the same last name. So you're looking over your shoulder; you're being careful. You have to use so much extra energy. It's a lot of extra stress.

Lisa: We're very lucky to live where we live.

Jennifer: Yes, you have to keep your eye on hope.

Lisa: This is just a portion of who we are.

Jennifer: But taxes and those different things about being married—things have to change at the Federal level. There was a couple that the one gal was getting deported after twelve years. They're married in California, but not federally. And immigration is federal. They have two children and she has to go back to the Philippines. These are the things you try to push aside. Prop. 8 was so stressful. We were scared. The family values group won. What about love and decency? We're the people that don't get seen—like Lisa and I. Like my grandma was saying, "Honey, how come I only see those people in all those parades? That's not who you are, is it? Are those who your friends are?" And that's how they see us when they don't know anybody who's gay. That's their image. But this is what it looks like, right here. It was disheartening on that one trip.

Lisa: There were these women who had been together forever—fifteen, twenty years, and some of them hadn't even met the other's parents. No holidays together. My grandmother was one of my favorite people, and I tried to have a conversation with her back in the days when Donahue was on TV, and every time there was a woman who was a lesbian that came on it would say, "Women who hate men," or something like that. Thinking back, that's what she was looking at. She was so sweet, she would say, "Oh honey, are you trying to tell me that you're lady-gay?" That somehow made it okay. I'd say, "Yeah, I think I am."

Jennifer: I can't wait for the day that young kids can just date. If I could have dated whomever I wanted it would have been a lot easier. It's no one's business. As much as we love each other, and we have a great life, we wouldn't choose it. It's just who you are. ■

Kathy

Kathy's a manager for a fairly large electronics company in the Silicon Valley area of California. No photo.

I'm in management. I've had to lay off a lot of people. It's really hard. I spent three days in the hospital recently from the stress. My blood pressure just dropped.

We move a lot of things overseas, but there are just some things we have to build and maintain over here. I spent a long time in China and they will surpass us. We can't just be a service economy. I just don't believe that's how we'll survive. We have to build something here. We're going to lose those skills—and that's one of the big problems. We're training the world. A lot of the Chinese come to college in the States. Everybody gets their education over here and then takes their skills back to their country. It really hurts me when we move things overseas that should stay here, because we do have better technical expertise and I don't want to see us giving everything away. My company had little choice about going overseas. Now there's an emerging middle class in China. They will be consumers. Frankly, I think the Internet is gradually leveling everything. People try to control it and restrict it and they can't. People are seeing what they could have. So, there will be a leveling in the next ten years.

As a consumer nation, we haven't learned to save. Everybody's expecting it to always be milk and honey—the Depression people understand it. I was raised as a Mormon and one of their teachings is to stock up; to have enough food and things so you could withstand tough times. I look at some of the people I laid off that live paycheck to paycheck and I think what are they going to do? It's heartbreaking sometimes.

I try to find people jobs. I'm a big softy. A lot of the people I've laid off have found jobs. That's the good news. One did not have anything and now he's had three offers this week. So things are picking up, at least in the electronics industry. Some people even got raises, but I think it's industry to industry. The automotive industry has got to be hell. It's scary. I worry. We're not being smart. We're complacent about it.

One of the things we did with our kids is make them travel. You ought to appreciate what you have, because it's not the same everywhere. Not even close. And I think that's one of the problems with our kids. They're so consumer-oriented, but they don't realize that that's not life.

Those are the things that worry me as a manager. It's tough. Not all managers are lining their pockets and screwing everybody over. They're trying to make a living just like everybody else. People care, though. You represent the company. You try to mitigate the damage, because if the company doesn't make it, then nobody does. ◼

Boulder Creek, California

Geoff

I live between two people named Geoff (see page 33). Both Geoffs have been my good neighbors since I moved to Boulder Creek nearly ten years ago.

I'm in IT [information technology]. I'm System Administrator at a large electronics company. Things are going pretty well. Except I've been trying to sell my house for three years.

There have only been a few layoffs; it hasn't been companywide. I got laid off from another large electronics company in 2001, not long after 9/11. It was a total bloodletting. They had layoff after layoff after layoff. Now the company is just a shadow of its former self. Where I'm at now is just a lot healthier.

Unlike the first layoffs, when the dot-com bubble burst, this has hit the computer industry a lot less hard. A lot of companies let so many people go the first time around that they're already running lean and mean.

I'm definitely right of center, but I'm not a crazy. I started out as a Democrat, as most younger people do. The first President I voted for was Carter. And something happened along the way—I grew up. But I have an open mind. I hope Obama's presidency succeeds, insofar as his success doesn't mean institutionalizing socialism, but I'm becoming disillusioned rapidly.

I'm sorry I don't have a lot of meat and potatoes to offer as far as horror stories about the economy are concerned. I'm lucky this time. I paid my dues last time. That was scary. I thought I was going to lose my house. In fact, I came very close to that. I was two years between jobs.

It was horrible. I went to several job fairs. There was just nothing. Right at the time I was laid off in 2001 that company had a job fair for us and there were long lines in front of every table. There were long conversations and it took forever to get through those lines—a lot of talking, handshakes, and gesticulating. I'd finally get to the front of the line and ask if they had anything in IT and they'd say no. And that was the end of it.

I got my current job by just watching the job boards. I started as a contractor. It was a real simple job, below my experience, but I grabbed it. It was coordinating the repair of the company's workstations. They had someone they'd contracted with to come in twice a day and perform hardware repairs. It was my job to take note of these cases and notify that third party. Their contract ran out and I said don't renew it—I can do that. Gradually, I took on more responsibilities and my job shifted to working on servers. ■

California's Central Valley

218

Washington, D.C.

Afterword

This is a collection of sundry observations from the road. I saw things that I could not photograph for various reasons (no place to pull the car over, permission not granted, general safety issues, or I simply forgot to take a photograph—yes, it happens).

Case studies are infinitely more interesting than the theories they are meant to support. Real people doing whatever-it-is-they-do allow all of us to play voyeur—after all that's where the story lies. That's where the characters are. That's where the rubber meets the road.

USA or Bust started out as my attempt to emulate Dorothea Lange and Studs Terkel; to wed them together in a harmonious marriage and present them to the world as one loving couple. Ostensibly, the book's focus was to be on the weak economy, but I allowed my interviewees free rein to talk about other things, such as politics and social issues. Where will the economy be by the time this book is published? We'll see. Plan for the worst; hope for the best.

There were pockets of the United States where I thought I might meet some anti-California sentiment. I imagine places like Arkansas and Tennessee have as many misconceptions about California as we do about them. Once on the road, I discovered that there's an odd, homogeneous blanket that's been drawn over this country in the past few decades—and it's smothered much of the regional character. Blame it on TV and movies, or maybe we just move around more than we used to, or maybe it's the national corporate chains everywhere, but cultural

220

bumps are gradually being flattened down. Yes, Little Rock, Arkansas is different from Portland, Oregon—but not by much. There are variants in cuisine and dialect, but not so much that any one place seemed far from home.

Quite a few people did not want to be photographed or recorded—even though they were more than willing to talk with me. I admit, I understand their reluctance. After all, I'm a stranger to them. I want to interview and photograph them for a book. I would probably say, "no," to me, too. I quickly learned to alleviate people's fears by letting them know I was not with the government or hitting them up for money. I'd hand them a business card, and this seemed to legitimize my presence. Once I had my foot in the door, most individuals happily participated. I was mildly surprised at the consistently polite manner in which I was treated. I never had a sense of being unsafe. And for all the miles I drove, I never had any close calls on the highway.

California

Los Angeles is a congested behemoth. I grew up in its sprawling suburbs from the fifties through the mid-seventies. Freeways were dense with cars when I left—now they are nearly impossible to navigate. The air has changed too, but only in the subtle shift of smoggy hues. At first blush the economy still seems fairly robust. At one large upscale shopping mall the expansive parking lot was filled to capacity.

Roughly halfway through my drive, I flew back to California for a 24-hour layover. My daughter was graduating from high school at a Middle College program. I've stayed on pretty good terms with my former father-in-law, who was in attendance with his sister. He's retired, and the economy is something he largely reads about in the newspaper.

That night I was close enough to get a ride back to my house. I slept in my own bed for the first time in over a month. Odd being back for just the night. The next morning I had breakfast with my daughter, then flew back to resume my drive. I got back to my sister's house in Virginia very late. Just driving back from the Washington Dulles Airport made me realize how dependent I'd grown on my ultrareliable GPS unit. The voice can be a little naggy at times: *"Turn left. Turn right. Go back. Recalculating. You're an idiot."*

Nevada

My stay in Las Vegas made me realize just how far outside of my comfort zone I was stretching. Vogue on the outside and vague on the inside, Las Vegas has no there there. Stopping in this shabby jewel reinforced my long-held belief that this town is a monument to all that is loud, obnoxious, and in bad taste in American society. One outstanding oddity (still in progress at the time of my visit) was City Center. A fantastically enormous complex of offices, retail outlets, and residential spaces along the Strip, it's architectural anchor-points are two leaning towers very reminiscent of the World Trade Towers frozen in collapse. Bad taste, indeed.

The Salvation Army is a great charitable organization, but they act very guarded when it comes to interviews (much like a real army). I first tried for an interview at one of their stores in California. That was a no go. The manager took my card and told me she'd have to clear it with her regional boss. In Las Vegas, I hit another wall in the bureaucracy that prevented me from interviewing the Public Relations guy—even though he was the PR guy. What better way to feel the pulse of the economy than to find out if the need for charity is up or down?

Stopped by Hoover Dam on my way out of town. The Colorado River Bridge is part of a major bypass project meant to take cars off the dam road. It had not quite linked up from canyon wall to canyon wall when I was there. It's scheduled to open near the end of 2010. Two competing wonders within stone-throwing distance of each other. Seems like a bad idea. Won't people want to slow down or stop their cars to look at Hoover Dam from the bridge? Could easily cause more problems than it solves. Maybe I *am* a pessimist.

Arizona

In Williams, there was a Roman Catholic Church across from my motel. As a former altar boy, I couldn't resist. It was near noon and the place was locked up tighter than Fort Knox. I knocked on every door, then I went around back to the rectory. I leaned on the doorbell several times. Nothing. Maybe it's just my imagination, but when I was a Catholic in good standing I thought that churches remained unlocked at all hours.

I also talked with a waitress at a Greek-Italian-American restaurant in Williams. She'd moved there not long ago to help her mother take care of her diabetic father.

Stopped later on my drive to see Barringer Meteor Crater. Impressive and thought-provoking. Back on the road, the landscape was flat and dry, with ridges and mountains in the far distance. I wondered if the impact that had formed that crater had anything to do with this vast desert region of the United States.

New Mexico

Thought I might be spending the night at a friend's rental property, but it was spoken for, so I pushed on. There, I said something about New Mexico.

Texas

Cut southeast from Amarillo (in the Texas Panhandle) along Route 287. The speed limit ranged from 70 MPH to half that for the small towns that dotted its path. One sweet woman in Claude ran an antique store, which is code for dust-collecting knickknacks. But she was the only deal in a town with a population of 1,400. The store had a Christian overtone to it, decked out with turquoise jewelry and homey decorative arts. The owner spoke in a friendly manner wrapped in soft-but-firm tones. I explained the purpose of my visit, but she was reluctant to allow me to record her or take her photograph. Throughout our conversation, I gently pressed her to allow me to record her, but she declined. She expressed concern for the country on many fronts. She talked largely about morality and ethics—and on this we agreed—they often seemed to be lacking in our social, corporate, political, and even religious leaders. The economy hadn't affected her adversely—a pattern that was emerging along my drive so far: the more rural, the slower things changed economically, while the more urban, the more people were hit harder and faster. Maybe country-centric people have always lived on the edge and within their means, and the more city-centric people push their limits. However, many of my pet theories evaporate upon deeper scrutiny. When I left the woman's shop, I had the sense that she was praying for me.

Somewhere between the Texas Panhandle and Dallas, there was a large herd of camels. No exit for miles—no way to safely stop and take photos. I was later told that they were used in movies.

Went by a payday loan place and was politely told no to an interview. The sole proprietor, a woman, appeared cautious as she unlocked the front door for me. I can't blame her—there's been some adverse publicity about this type of money-lending operation as of late—especially with the sinking economy.

I spoke very briefly with a very busy Dr. Daniel (Doctor Dan, the Medicine Man). He's the local pharmacist in a suburb of Dallas. He's been in business there just shy of thirty years. He ran with the bulls in Pamplona, Spain some years back—and appears no worse for wear. A few years earlier than that, he wrestled a burglar into submission at his place of business until the police arrived. Quite the stud. I watched him in action with his customers. Gentle with children as he gave them their vaccinations and helpful with customer's needs, he is one of those people who anchors his community.

Stopped by a church in the evening when their Angel Food program was to take place. I talked with the pastor's wife and she politely took my business card. Her husband was preparing for a church service and she didn't want to be interviewed.

Arkansas

Through Arkansas (so why is it not pronounced R-Kansas?) and Tennessee just off Interstate 40, there was a healthy dose of churches and adult superstores. Also, fewer Spanish-language radio stations in the middle of America. *Mi Dios!*

In Hot Springs, I spent the night in an especially non-aromatic, half-star motel. It rained all night. And it was still raining in the morning when I checked out. Downtown was blocked to traffic by the local constabulary. I don't know why. I used an alternate route and drove straight to Little Rock, where I stopped for a bite to eat.

There was one other couple at the diner. The man was talking on his cell phone, telling the person on the other end how to create a blog that would link up to his prayer site. Two younger guys were across the room taking photographs of the food for the owner. I kept thinking they needed more light than that provided by the small overhead restaurant bulb. But then, they didn't ask me.

Saw the William J. Clinton Presidential Center. There's a full-scale re-creation of the oval office—much smaller than I had imagined. Talked with a family about California, where they are considering moving.

Tennessee

I stayed outside Nashville at a chain motel whose bright, tall sign states that rooms start at $31.99. Inside my room a card on the door had the price as $59.99. Has the current economy cut the price nearly in half or is this a seasonal difference? That's the hard part: what areas of society have regularly bordered on sinking below the poverty line and which ones are very much affected by the current economic downturn?

I tried to interview the friendly lady who had checked me in, but another woman stepped in and said she couldn't, for corporate reasons. I should have seen this one coming. The boss-woman who took charge had a Chihuahua that sniffed me, thought about it, then yipped. That should have been the giveaway. And just what are "corporate reasons?"

Nashville's section of the Cumberland River was running high in May. It had swallowed up a whole lower level of the waterfront at the end of Broadway. Flagpoles capped by colored pennants poked up through the fluid surface like giant cattails isolated from the shore. The upper dry levels seemed reserved for the down and out. They looked identical to the down-and-out that pepper society even during a robust economy.

At a Waffle House, not far outside Nashville, a man sitting near me at the breakfast bar had a voice ranging between that of the late Paul Harvey and that of Red Sovine. He had the dismissive tone of authority earned through hard work. He wore his politics on his sleeve, as he schooled his wife in the ways of the world with a judgmental shake of the head. Maybe I should have talked with him.

The Waffle House chain is a throwback to the restaurants of yesteryear: thick-walled coffee mugs, a decidedly non-heart-smart menu, and older, bouffant-haired waitresses who call you, "Hon." A woman of retiree age, sitting next to me at the counter, talked about federalized health care and how she was against it. She told me how her husband had just gone to the VA for a foot injury and was turned away—being told to come back in one week. I thought it seemed like an inexpensive way of determining if his foot was broken or just sprained. *Come back in a week and we'll know for sure.* But considering the woman's anti-national health care stance, I nodded in tactful agreement.

Man, oh man. Elvis! Maybe he was Jesus' second coming and we just didn't see it. *But I digress.* Graceland is operated just like any other well-run amusement park. The corporate machine lines and loads everybody up just across the street, then buses everybody over. The house is not all that big. And it illustrates my belief that wealth simply magnifies one's bad taste (or maybe, Las Vegas rubbed off on him?) Graceland is tacky, gaudy, and chintzy. He might have been the King, but he had no decorative sense. And just why is there no Elvis impersonator greeting you at the door? Mr. Presley had some great songs, gyrations, and performances, but his cozy home is now a mausoleum to kitsch—as dead as the man himself.

I've been rebuked by some interesting people—for example, an African American woman, Jacqueline, who was petitioning for better use of the Dr. King site, right outside the Lorraine Motel in Memphis. I'm pretty sure she saw me as an interloper, and was very reluctant to talk with me. She was joined by a mountain of a black guy who regarded me with even less favor. He, too, did not want to be interviewed or photographed.

Virginia

I watched an open-heart bypass surgery take place at my sister's hospital while waiting to interview Alan, the cardiac surgeon. The hospital is on Gallows Road. Really. Reminds me of a physician I had whose last name was Posthumus. Really.

One morning I stopped by the National Museum of the Marine Corps. Impressive architecture—a worthy monument to some very brave men and women. Bought a bottle of Jarhead Red wine for later enjoyment. A product of California, thank you very much.

There's a six-year-old greasy spoon I visited. I was hoping for an interview with the eponymous owner. Apparently, he had sold the business a few years earlier, and there's no such person there. So I chatted with Janet, who was serving coffee.

According to the testimony of two women sitting nearby, Janet is the heart and soul of the diner. If she were to go elsewhere, they would follow. It was past the breakfast rush, so Janet had some time. She absolutely did not want to be recorded, because she was afraid of freezing up. I agreed, and just listened. Her husband's a painter/renovator, and his business has dropped off severely. Together they'd bought a rental property a year or so earlier, but found it was a losing proposition, so they wanted to do a short sale with a prominent bank. The bank refused, foreclosed on them, then sold the house at auction for one-third of what they would have received in the short sale.

A woman popped her head out from the kitchen and said she'd talk with me, but we'd have to set up some time for later. Her name was Susan. I said "Great, that's my ex-wife's name." And we immediately hit it off. She was usually the other waitress, but was filling in for Blanca, who, according to the signs posted around the diner, was recovering from leg surgery, and could we donate money to the cause? Both Susan and Blanca are single mothers working hard. If they don't work, they don't get paid. And the cost of surgery and hospitalization could not be covered by the diner.

Susan had to get back to cooking, but gave me a contact number. As I was finishing up with my breakfast, two men at the far end of the diner got up to leave. One tapped me on the arm as he passed by and said that his ex-wife's name was Susan, too.

Susan never did meet with me, but by now I was getting used to the variety of ways people say no.

Washington, D.C.

I drove into D.C. early. I was hoping to park outside of town and ride the Metro in, but I got a little turned around. When I finally had my bearings back, the Washington Monument loomed closely on the horizon, so I just found a parking spot a few blocks from the Lincoln Memorial Reflecting Pool and hoofed it the rest of the way. Rolling Thunder was in town for their 22nd Annual motorcycle ride. They form a large army of veterans and others who want accountability for service people Missing In Action or who are Prisoners Of War. I talked briefly with a few of them and got some photos.

Maryland

A Luddite view of life always baffles me. Where does one draw the end of the timeline? 1941? 1800? The good-natured Amish shopkeeper in Maryland had adopted an obvious cessation of progress, but only in certain areas. I'm pretty sure his family was using an electric cash register for the transactions. It was not until a few days later that I began to wonder about how he might get all his wares to his weekend market? By buggy? Wagon?

Delaware

Visiting my former brother-in-law Steve and his wife Carol in Delaware. It's been ten years. Two bottles of wine later and we were pretty much caught up. We talked politics, social injustice, and, of course, the economy.

Lower Delaware is referred to as "slower Delaware"— which is where I went to interview people at a NASCAR race.

Pennsylvania

At a renowned cheese steak eatery in Philadelphia, there were three old mob-like guys outside at a table waxing poetical about the good old days. The loudest of the group, who was holding court, sounded like Joe Pesci. You had the sense that he was a small fish in a small pond whose life was only elevated by telling tales about the way the neighborhood used to be and about self-aggrandizing youthful feats of derring-do—real or imagined. The group was straight out of central casting. I enjoyed eavesdropping. Great local color.

New York

A sign on the Brooklyn Bridge as you enter Brooklyn reads: *How sweet it is!* The one exiting Brooklyn on the Williamsburg Bridge reads: *Oy Vey!* Apparently all the signs in and out of this particular borough are intended for comic relief.

I didn't get on Cash Cab, one of my minor regrets. Now the nation will not see just how little I know. It seems like every day I learn more and more about less and less. Pretty soon I'll know everything about nothing.

I paid my respects at the World Trade Center site, then I took the *Miss New York* ferry *(How can you miss New York if you don't leave?)* to Liberty Island and Ellis Island. I got my Swiss Army knife confiscated—that's two in less than a year. I should buy stock. You'd think I would have learned, with heightened security everywhere.

NYC seemed least like home. Don't get me wrong, I love New Yorkers, maybe I was just worn out from traveling. A subway agent told me to, "Take the A train." Made me think of Duke Ellington. I couldn't get that tune out of my head until I returned to Brooklyn and got lost. Damn you, New York!

I flagged down the one cabbie (not the Cash Cab) that didn't know his streets or have a map. We stopped three times to ask for directions. People along the route were very helpful, and I eventually got back to my motel. In the cabbie's defense, he'd only been in the country six months and he lived in Queens, not Brooklyn. Maybe the cab company should pony up a little money for a GPS unit. They'd make their money back in a day. The ride through Brooklyn reminded me of being in a Third World country—a little broken, a little sad, just holding on. Lots of Puerto Rican flags—very few U.S. I'm just saying that once you make the decision to live in the United States, your country of origin should take a backseat to your adopted homeland. Okay. Putting away my soapbox.

On one Manhattan-bound subway car, a mariachi quartet launched into a ranchero ballad. This really only works when the car is half full, and it was. The music was lively. I donated some money to the cause when one of them came around passing the hat. I'm always a sucker for the arts. The group quickly departed to the next car and repeated their performance for those weary travelers. I guess this way, the band only needs to know one song. Going between cars is clearly labeled "prohibited," but it's posted in English— a language barely spoken in New York, even by the natives. So maybe I'm in the minority. Anyway, I do really love all the flavors presented in this great, dynamic city in this great, dynamic country.

On Wall Street, a female police officer gave me the once-over as she sat in the passenger side of a parked patrol car—but it was more with suspicion than interest. You know: single, swarthy male with beard and camera. He must be up to no good. And here I was thinking she was a good-looking gal in uniform. But one of my minor goals on this trip was to not get rousted by the man (or, in this case, the woman), so I moved on.

Got up one morning with the intent of taking a large sign to Wall Street saying, "Talk to me about the economy." Thought better of it. Carrying a big stand and placard on the subway might be frowned upon. As it turned out, the cars were jammed, and my choice was sound. Anyway, I talked with two young stockbrokers on break standing on Wall Street. The older one is in his mid-twenties, the younger just eighteen. They work with a group of 120 other brokers, manning phones, making the money move. Neither wanted to be photographed or recorded, but they were willing to talk with me. The older broker did the lion's share. He told me the last six months had been bad and he thought the stock market had bottomed out back in March. It seemed to be floating up gradually, but it was soft. About President Obama's efforts, he commented that a trillion dollars had better do something. His predictions for the near future of finance were dire. He believes the economy hasn't even been hit by credit card debt yet, and that things would get worse.

Before hitting Wall Street, I'd stopped by City Hall, where people were gathering outside on the steps for an upcoming press conference. I was up front with two of New York's Finest, and confessed that I wasn't really press—but it's funny how carrying a big camera around gives that impression. They wouldn't let me in, but happily talked with me. I gave them my business card. The tall one told me a brief history of the building and grounds. The other looked at my card and said he'd hitchhiked around California in his misspent youth.

My subway ride back to my base of operations in Brooklyn filled me with the sights, sounds, and smells of greater New York. There's a bittersweet stale, odor consisting of two parts sweat and one part urine that permeates the underground platforms as the heat builds with the addition of each new waiting body. You're ready to forswear your beliefs and pray to any god for relief when you feel the breeze of the incoming train as it pushes the air through the tunnel into the station. Once you're on board, a certain noninteractive protocol takes over. Never make eye contact. Mind your own business. Stare at something, anything, as long as it's not human. Act disinterested in life. If you're lucky, what passes for air-conditioning is actually working, and you've found a seat and settled into a stupor for the ride.

New Jersey & Pennsylvania (again)

Farewell to New York City, my turnaround spot. Last night there was bright lightning and explosive thunder. This morning I waited for the rain to recede, then drove over the Williamsburg Bridge, across Manhattan, down the Holland Tunnel, and I was out of there. New Yorkers are generally a lovable bunch, but I was still happy to leave the place. Got through New Jersey without incident and stopped in western Pennsylvania to rest my tired backside.

A few miles earlier, when I'd pulled over for gas, I'd wondered out loud to the woman working the register why a Citgo station wouldn't accept Citgo credit cards, as their sign said—not that I had one, just wondering. The woman said they were going independent soon so they could make more money. As it stood now, they made only three cents on every gallon of gasoline they sold. Not much of a profit margin, no matter how much volume they do.

Ohio

Something amusing at the Rock and Roll Hall of Fame and Museum in Cleveland: among the relics and residue of rock sits Rick James' Rickenbacker bass complete with discolored linear burn on its head. Musicians often tuck their cigarettes in under the string and headstock between puffs so they have their hands free to play. I chuckled a little too loudly, which earned me a sour look from one of the other patrons.

Indiana

Sorry Indiana, I've got nothing.

Wisconsin

Hung out with a few of my former family members: Cy, Bill, and Christie. They usually give me a hard time about being from California, and I remind them about the book, *Wisconsin Death Trip.* Cy is my aforementioned ex-father-in-law. His "real" first name is Adolph—a name not all that popular during World War II, at least not for our side. There's a photo of him and a fellow G.I. burning a Nazi flag in Vienna, so he aces, in my book.

There's a painting in a Milwaukee art museum by Christian Ludwig Bokelmann (German 1844 – 1894), *The People's Bank Shortly Before the Crash, 1877,* depicting a long line of darkly-dressed, sour-looking people waiting for the bank to open. Crashes happen. During the Great Depression of the 1930s, the song of hope was, "Happy Days are Here Again." We could use some uplifting ditty for the soundtrack of our current predicament.

Illinois

Stopped in Chicago during a heavy downpour for just a few hours, then left. Oprah never returned my calls.

Iowa

In Iowa I put my feet in the waters of the Mississippi, just so I could write about it now. A feat (pun intended) I will not be able to repeat, since one can't step in the same river twice. This was on my return drive, going west. I totally zoned out when I crossed the mighty river the first time, heading east. It must have been on that long, metal-grated bridge, but there were many trees obscuring my side view.

The breakfast area of a motel was packed with a small army of retirees. Blue- and gray-haired, uniform in style, catalog-casual clothes. I had my bagel and coffee in silence and took in life's rich pageant.

Madison County—didn't see any bridges.

Nebraska

Stopped to take photographs along interstate 80. Lots of quirky roadside Americana.

Wyoming

When I was eating at a McDonald's off Interstate 80 in Rock Springs, two young men walked in wearing service industry uniforms. The names stitched above their pockets were Levi and Jeremiah. I was an hour and a half from Utah.

Utah

In the dark, while driving, I caught glimpses of the moonlight reflected off the massive Great Salt Lake. Outside the cones of my headlight beams the rest of the landscape lay in eerie blackness.

Idaho

Drove like a madman. My goal was to drive from Wyoming to Oregon in one mighty chunk. Don't know why. It just seemed right at the time. Nearing the end of my trip, I felt like a horse racing back to the stable.

Oregon

Put in almost 1,100 miles in one big bite. Just inside the state line a Highway Patrol car pulled me over. Thought I was busted for going 68 in a 65, but he stopped me because my one headlight had gone dim. He asked where I was coming from and I told him that was an interesting question. I showed him the map of my drive and he chuckled. It explained the *USA or Bust!* written on my back bumper. No ticket. Phew! I made it to Portland, dim headlight and all.

A few days later, I talked with a young woman at a local watering hole. She'd recently joined her family business, building large commercial structures nationwide. Things have slowed, not for lack of work, but for the trickle-down process of banks loaning out money to the people who want their buildings built.

California (back home)

I attended a Fourth of July parade and party that I was invited to (thanks Michael) because of some local publicity about my *USA or Bust* project. I interviewed several people about their lives and the economy.

General

On my drive, I only listened to whatever was on the radio. No CDs or tapes. I figured I'd pick up more local color that way. It seemed more authentic. Besides, my tape deck was broken and I had no CD player. I heard a lot of radio preachers: loud and mighty—absolute in their certainty. Unwavering in their condemnations. Rush Limbaugh has the central rural radio markets sewn up. Sometimes I could hear him proselytizing the rabid Right's distortion of reality on three separate overlapping stations. And he wasn't the worst. But it kept me awake with anger and entertainment. And believe me, the far Left is just as bad. But they have fewer radio stations in the middle of our nation.

There are a lot of Vietnam-era veterans out riding motorcycles. The convergence of retirement and VA benefits? Now they get to see the country they fought for. Also saw scads of pickup trucks and big rigs—sometimes triple rigs.

I did not contract Swine Flu, have my flesh eaten by a bacteria or virus, get bitten by bed bugs, or become deranged by Mad Cow Disease. I was not attacked by killer bees. And just whatever happened to acid rain? So many worries, so little time.

No photo—well, no good photo—an older East-Indian woman in a traditional *sari,* with her husband in tow at the San Jose Airport carrying a large "Sale – Victoria's Secret" bag. Just what was she wearing under that *sari?* Cultures embracing, not clashing.

Another *sari* sight for sore eyes: One driver I saw at a rest stop was also a gray-haired Indian woman in a *sari.* She hoisted herself up into the cab of a Peterbilt and drove off too quickly to catch for an interview. It reminded me of the time I saw four Asian Buddhist monks in orange robes shopping at a Costco and I didn't have a camera.

The weather was largely cooperative. The worst lasted the shortest. I missed seeing any tornadoes—don't know what I would have done in the middle of nowhere had I seen one.

I didn't do much in the way of nightlife (maybe that's another book?). I was usually worn out by day's end after having driven, walked, photographed and interviewed people.

Not as many rebel flags as I thought there would be—especially in the South.

Lots of sneaky State Patrol cars parked in hidden alcoves along the highway waiting to pounce—revenue enhancement at its finest.

Off the side of the road: a man on a horse stopped to talk with somebody in a pickup. Almost a Norman Rockwell painting.

There was an antebellum house off Interstate 40 in Tennessee with a TV dish attached.

Every exit has a McDonald's or every McDonald's has an exit? Discovered that they aren't allowed to call their larger meals *super-sized* after the movie came out.

Motivation for trip: escape, adventure, art, money, self-discovery.

Most cheap motels have cigarette burns on bed covers, even though these are smoke-free rooms.

Punishing Recession: no one wants to use the D-word. R-word will suffice (and I don't mean Democrat or Republican).

Life is filled with more opportunities to fail than succeed. I don't know why it's not talked about more. It's always easier to handle success than failure. Actually, that's not true. Many a good success has been squandered by its owner. On this trip, I suspect that some people did not want to talk to me because they were embarrassed by their financial fall from grace during this downturn.

Signs of the time: Blues Festival in Chicago 2009—usually four days, cut to three this year due to the economy. After almost forty years, Artweek, a West Coast art review and resource magazine, closed up shop in June. At my bank, Chase (previously Washington Mutual, previously Great Western), in mid-July, "Registered warrants issued by the state of California are no longer accepted." In late 2007, an E-trade on-line savings account was at 5% interest; two years later it's 0.6% —nearly a 90% free fall.

A few dead armadillos on the highways and byways of Texas and Arkansas. Strange critters, especially when flattened.

Back East, before tollbooths, there are signs saying, "Check Brakes." Good idea.

Heart of American farmland: I never did see one crop circle.

Continental Divide. Didn't stop to check the flow of water east or west.

It was always an excitement to arrive somewhere—to see it looming in the near distance: New York City's or Chicago's skyline, the Washington Monument poking up along the horizon, a landmark of some prominence becoming real outside my car's windshield.

Winding down: There were those I met on the road who expressed serious doubts about the future of the United States—that we had peaked, that our best days were behind us, that all empires crumble and fall, that we were on the decline. I don't buy it. Believing is seeing. And I believe the United States is still in its infancy, and we have a long, productive life ahead of us. Conversely, I also believe that we are mortgaging our children and grandchildren's future with our quick-fix remedies to our economic problems—we've been doing it for decades.

Despite our problems, the United States is still a beacon of hope for much of the world. I once worked with a great guy who had immigrated here with his wife from Romania when it was still a communist country. They did not have any children, because they did not want to raise them under the specter of communism. They went through various degrees of grief to get here. They had to find a sponsor. They were followed by Romanian secret police. Needless to say, getting to the U.S. was not easy. Finally, with all the paperwork settled, they boarded a plane to fly here. One of the flight attendants heard about what they were doing and brought them champagne. A fellow passenger reached into his pocket and pulled out several hundred dollars. Handing it to them he said, "Welcome to America."

Okay, now I really will put away my soapbox. ▪

The Author and his trusty 2001 Hyundai Accent

For technophiles, I used two digital photo cameras made by Sony:

The Big Gun -
Alpha A-900 DSLR (24.6 megapixels of raw power) with a SAL-2470Z Carl Zeiss
Vario-Sonnar f2.8 24-70mm Zoom Lens

The Spy Cam -
DSCW300 (13.6 megapixels and fits in the palm of the hand)

www.atomicdroppress.com

www.ingramcontent.com/pod-product-compliance
Lightning Source LLC
Chambersburg PA
CBHW041221270326
41932CB00006B/41